My Father, the Sea and Me

By Captain Judy Helmey

Typesetting and Design by:

Lauren Clackum
Pacific Publishers, LLC
PO Box 2813, Tybee Island, Georgia 31328

Print ISBN: 979-8-88617-025-2

Printed in the United States of America

My father, Captain Sherman I. Helmey.

DEDICATION

For over forty years, my father has been involved in the charter boat industry. I have watched him entertain people with his stories about all his adventures in the thirties and all his fish tales there after.

He loved fishing and spending time with people. Every fishing day was like his first. His enthusiasm never seemed to leave him.

I am dedicating this book to him in hopes that these stories he told may live on. My only regret is, I wished I had written down all his stories. I have to write most of these by memory. Thank Goodness, he repeated them often!

So, here's to you Dad, your stories will always have a chance to live on and that wonderful smile you had while you were telling them might still live on in other people.

Your daughter Judy.

Captain Judy Helmey.

ABOUT MY BOOK

I am not an author, nor do I claim to be. However I am very interested in getting you to read my book. I want to share with you the many secrets that lie beyond the boundaries of land! Those secrets that stretch far out into the ocean.

My friends wanted me to have a ghost writer to read and change the way I have chosen to write my book. I felt that I wanted to say it my way. I know that it might not be done in the best grammar, but it is me speaking from the heart!

This book is about the life I spent with my father. By the way, I wouldn't say he was normal. He led a great adventurous life. I was lucky enough to spend time with him and all his amazing happenings. Its about things he did in the thirties before I arrived and times we spent together after the fifties. He was a very good fisherman. I carry on a family business that was very much a part of him and is very much a part of me. I love it as much as he did. So I choose fishing to be my life, too!

This is not a book just about fishing. It's about sunken ships, mermaids, Al Capone, and many more likely and unlikely events my father has come across.

I have seen most of what I have written about. The rest my father told me about. I want to share all these wonderful stories with you.

CAPTAIN JUDY HELMEY

Captain Judy shows off her catch.

ABOUT THE AUTHOR

I was fortunate to be able to try different things in my life and to be able to decide in which direction I wanted my future to head. I can remember from the time I was young, I was making my own decision. They may have been small, but they were mine.

Being raised by one parent has it's advantages and disadvantages. Luckily, I can say it worked out to my advantage. I seem to have the same interests as my father. As time went on, I was able to get a taste for other ways of life; but I always came back to fishing.

Fishing isn't just a sport or a pass time for me, its even more than just a business. It's my life. I get all my strength from it. I have been taking people fishing for twenty-five years. What I have experienced and the people I have met and spent time with is priceless. I guess you could say that my customers make up the Miss Judy's Fishing Team.

I hope to continue my fishing career. One day I want to be considered the best at what I do.

With all the new changes, new rules and changing regulations; I think fishing will only get better. Old fishing ideas of catching them all today and leaving none for tomorrow are disappearing. The now fishermen are ready for the changes.

I wish I had twenty-five more years, but I know that could never happen. No matter how many years I have left, I look forward to them with a smile on my face.

TABLE OF CONTENTS

1. My Father And Me 1
2. Fascinating Stories My Father Told........................ 29
3. Powers That Be 37
4. Full Moon Adventures 39
5. Junk Yard Monkey 41
6. Rattlesnakes And Rabbits 43
7. Dead Bodies.. 45
8. Mullet Jumping.. 47
9. Summer Camp.. 49
10. Judy's Eighty Pound Cobia 53
11. Mystery Sea 57
12. Amazing Discoveries Of Sharks 59
13. King Neptune.. 61
14. The Captain Is A Lady.. 63
15. Captain Ali Young (1955-2021) 67
16. Captain Bill Marsh (1935-2013)............................ 73
17. Finding The Barnstable 77
18. Rumors Began To Fly 87
19. Georgia State Records.. 89
20. Intriguing Fish 113
21. Enticing Bottom Baits.. 117
22. Chopper Blues 121
23. Fish Do The Darndest Things 123
24. Playing The Fish.. 125
25. Feathered Friends And Their 127
26. Extraordinary Past 127
27. Predicting Weather Natures Way.......................... 131
28. Twenty-Two Years Later.. 135

29. Murphy's Law 139

30. St Elmo's Fire 143

31. Ride The Wild Catfish............................... 145

32. Small Boats/Big Fish............................... 147

33. Disaster At Sea 149

34. Kung-Fu Fishing..................................... 153

35. Just Say No.. 155

36. The Underwater Stalker 157

37. Shark Attack.. 159

38. The Sea Monster 165

39. Sounds From The Deep 169

40. Captain Judy's Recipes.......................... 173

41. Got More Books!!!................................... 175

My father and me.

MY FATHER AND ME

My father was born on July 22, 1902, in Effingham County, just west of Savannah. His full name is Sherman Israel Helmey. I have never heard anyone call him Israel, always Sherman.

His family owned a big farm in a place he always referred to as "Scuffle Town." Each of the children helped work the farm. According to Randall, my father's brother, he would do anything to get out of doing his share. When we would go to Uncle Randall's house, it was always a joke at the dinner table. Daddy was much stronger and bigger, and he made poor Uncle Randall do a lot of his chores. I got to know a few of his brothers and sisters.

I was a late baby. I was born when my father was 51 years old. His sister, Mrs. J.F. Zipperer, was not just an aunt to me, she was more like my grandmother. Aunt Hattie was a fine southern lady. Everyone always listened to what she had to say except Daddy. He wouldn't listen when she told him he needed to slow down and not party so much. Aunt Hattie called all the ladies he dated "PEACOCKS" (not a bird but a female). Of course, he would laugh and still go on dating the same as usual. I can remember that most of all about him. He did pretty much what he wanted, when he wanted to.

My father's younger brother, Mac Helmey, was quite a sport. Uncle Mac was the baby of the family. He owned the first lumber company in Savannah. I never knew any of the other brothers and sisters. I was very young when they past away.

Well, from what I told you, Daddy wasn't much for farming life. I'm sure there were other people involved in helping him with his chores.

When his parents purchased their first car is when my father knew he wasn't going to be a farmer, but an automobile mechanic. I guess you could say that the invention of the car caused many changes and he was right there to change with it.

The family car was definitely a hit with my father. He loved to take it apart to see how it was put together. Aunt Hattie used to tell me that he wouldn't do anything but work on that car. He

1

Helmey's Garage located on Drayton Street.

would tell his father it was broke and he would have to work on it all day just to get it running again. Aunt Hattie would always say, "Sherman you know how that car got broke, you did it when taking it apart." My father seem to always get his way when it came to that automobile. He just couldn't seem to take his mind off the car much less his hands. He was always under the hood doing something.

According to Aunt Hattie, he had another trick. He would tell his father the car was broken. Of course, it was not. His brothers would always say "Sherman doesn't want us to use the car." When he knew someone was going to drive it, he would put a gas soaked rag in the carburetor. When they turned the car switch on, the rag would ignite and blow the hood off. This would put daddy in back in the driver seat once again.

In the early thirties, my father decided to leave home. He had enough of the farming life. He told me that his mother gave him $25.00. He took the money and off he went to find his future in the big city.

This must have been a horrifying experience for him, setting out into a world he knew nothing about. Although, he did know about automobiles and what made them work, so he went to the first car repair shop he came to and asked for a job. Of course, they laughed and asked, "Where did you get your experience?" He replied, "At home taking the family car apart and putting it back together." Well, with that statement, there didn't seem to be any jobs available in the area.

My father decided to try a new approach. The next owner, he would offer his services for a week with no set pay. At the end of the week, an agreement would be made as to whether or not he would have the job. This enabled my father to secure a job without pay for a week. He knew as soon as they saw how good he could repair cars, the would hire him. He worked for a week and did the work of three people. He was hired. He could disassemble and reassemble a whole care in two days.

With his new job, he had one thing in mind. He had to work hard and save his money so he could go into business for himself. He did this. He called his business "Helmey's Garage."

Pete Hudson and my father (nicknamed "Moose") owned Hudson-Helmey Garage located on Montgomery Street.

The rest of the store is HEARSAY or maybe it's the TRUTH.

Somewhere between his old job and his new business, he got married. This was his first marriage. They were gifted with a baby girl. They named her Merceles.

"Helmey's Garage" seemed to be doing well. My father had devised several different methods for making the automobile more comfortable. He took the shocks and added shoe leather to them to cushion the bumps. He told me that General Motors used his idea in their shock system. He had lots of business and people were always happy to let him try his new ideas on their cars. I am sure this was good as long as the ideas worked.

One day a man walked in and asked my father if he would like to build some special cars for him. Of course, my father being in the car repair business said, "Yes, I would love to." And he did. They made a deal. He would be doing some traveling to General Motors to pick up these new cars.

My father's job was to pick the cars up, bring them back to his shop, and repair them as ordered. He was to make them appear not loaded down, even when they could hold no more! He was to build compartments in unnoticeable places where cargo could not be seen. He gave these cars a nickname called "Shoe Salesman" cars. I have no idea where this nickname came from. He was to store these cars before and after their use. He had lots of extra space on the third floor of his building.

These cars were taken to Wilmington Island to a known spot and were to await a shipment of shoes. I guess! The spot was a speakeasy located at the southeast end of the island. This spot had easy access from the river. When transporting took place, there was always a party going on. Lots of people and cars would be there. The shoes were picked up by rowboat captains then delivered to the location. Sometimes these shoes were even thrown overboard into the mud. This would happen if the rowboat did not make the rendezvous on time. The rowboats picked up the cargo and delivered it to the proposed spot. They pulled up under a part of the building that hung over the water. The cargo was then passed through a trap door in the floor and transferred to the cars that my father built. Yes, Wilmington Island was certainly a popular place!

There was a large hotel built. The "Oglethorpe" was quite a large hotel for it's time. There were always plenty of people staying there that had business son the island. Some very important people in the underworld used to frequent this place.

The man my father supposedly worked with was "Big Al" Capone and the shoes he was supposed to be hauling was short for cases of whiskey. I think? I'm not sure about all of this, I wasn't there. However I am sure about "Helmey's Garage." I have pictures to prove it.

Of course, as with any business, hauling whiskey had its problems. The police were suppose to turn their heads and not see what was happening. This worked fine for awhile. As styles changed and others got involved, these special cars were beginning to be hard to recognize. My father had to come up with another idea. He did. He designed a tire with certain markings which would give these cars a certain look. Now, once again, they were in business.

The police were working on the other side of town on the night the shoe deliveries were to take place. If they were to see something not quite right, they could look at the tires before stopping the car.

Charlie Eden painting on of "Big Al's" cars.

6

My father's life appeared to be going pretty well. Some where between the "Shoe Salesman" cars and the ride to General Motors, his first wife left him. Taking with her his pride and joy, his only daughter, Merceles.

I never knew any certain dates. All I know is that it would have happened the way my father said, "We are now living on Wilmington Island and I have been since I was born." Now why would a country boy with no past on the water be so interested in living on the water?

My father was lucky. He was able to grab a part of time that we are only able to read about. A time where things didn't seem rushed and complicated. I know he wasn't doing the right thing by being a part of all the whiskey hauling. Although, it does sound very exciting to me! I couldn't say that I wouldn't have tried myself. After all, maybe it might not be true, he might have just dreamed it up!

After all the changes in my father's life, his new business, the divorce, he started living a little. He had many women friends. You know "PEACOCKS." One of the most familiar names I remember was LILLA BLAND. My father always mentioned her. I never got to meet her in person, but she did call a while back to ask about daddy. She seemed to be very nice on the phone. I wish I could have met her in person.

My father was flying high, he had plenty of money, lots of dates and things were going smoothly. He was still doing some travelling up north to pick cars up. He also went south to do some visiting. He had purchased a forty foot yacht. Off to Florida he would go to visit STAR ISLAND. This was the island where "Big Al" lived and played on. My father docked his boat there while he visited. He always talked about all the parties and all the people that were involved. Names of people I wish I had wrote down, but didn't.

My father retired from the automobile business in the early fifties. About this time, he met another woman, Jerry. They got married. Jerry is my mother. This would be his second marriage. He was still paying alimony from his first marriage. This would go on for forty five years.

My mother, Jerry, standing on the bow of the Miss Jerry

I always wondered why he paid alimony for so long. I found out later in life the reason. My father always told me the judge and lawyers decided this was the thing for him to do. In the early days, divorces were not as acceptable to society. This meant he would pay. Well, I never understood why he had to pay so much. He always said, "We were only married for a few years." I finally figured it out the day I got a copy of the divorce papers. He had been married to his first wife over twenty years. It was a true shock to me. My father, on the other hand, must have had a lapse of memory…

After my father married Jerry, they travelled a lot on his yacht, the "Miss Jerry." I know they had their problems. My father was in his late forties and my mother was in her early twenties. Since my father was retired, they always had plenty of time to travel. They traveled south during the winter and north during the summer. They also spent a lot of time on the barrier islands, located just off our coast, such as Wassaw, Little Tybee, and Daufuskie Island. They must have had a great time. He would always take the fish and shrimp they caught and cook them on the spot. He even talked about the times they would run aground and have to stay there until the tide came in. That's something I would never have admitted to. The "Miss Jerry" was a boat of its time.

She was a forty-foot yacht with lots of space. They were very comfortable traveling up and down the coast on her. I had not arrived yet, so there wasn't anything to tie them down.

Seven years after their marriage, they had a little girl. November 13, 1951, Judy Lynn Helmey was born. Yes, of course, this was me. I was almost born on a boat. My mother and father were leaving on a weekend trip to Wassaw. Before leaving, my mother had been to the doctor and he told her it would be weeks before I was born, so they thought they had plenty of time to go. However, something happened. My mother was in the store, and I decided to show up early. She was rushed to the hospital. I was almost born before the arrival at the hospital. My father had been out shopping for the trip and when he returned, I had arrived. The first of many travels I caused to be postponed.

As soon as I was born we moved from downtown Savannah to Wilmington Island. This was all against my mother's will. She liked living in town best, she thought, until she moved to the island. After the move, she never wanted to cross the river. Believe me, I don't either. A lot of people feel that way. Island living is the best!

Miss Judy's famous hold up.

Miss Judy's famous pose.

We still traveled on the yacht. The only changes made was to add a crib, which by the way, they should have put a top on. On one boat outing I managed to get out of the crib. My mother caught me just before I crawled over the side of the yacht.

My mother adapted quite well to island living. She started selling live bait and did very well at it. My father would catch them and she would sell them. The "Miss Jerry" stayed at home more and more as I started walking. This is when "Helmey's Charter Boat" business was started. Friends who had been going out with my father and mother on their trips still wanted to go. They came up with a price and the next thing you knew, my father was taking people fishing and charging them. There weren't a lot of trips but he has other interests too. He had to provide bait for my mom to sell and I think he was still fixing up wrecked cars. He still has to mess with cars, he loved it.

The "Miss Jerry" was sitting at the dock more and more. They were not able to spend as much time on her as before. My father had taken some trips and there were still calls coming in. he knew what he would have to do if he was going to continue

10

Captain Helmey and fishing party.

using the "Miss Jerry" for charter. She wasn't built for fishing, she was a luxury yacht. She didn't have much open aft room. He needed more open space for fishing so he made some changes.

He took a skill saw and cut the wonderful "Miss Jerry's" cabin off. The two double beds located in the cabin were now in the cockpit. Of course, he changed them into seats. After all, the people needed a place to sit and fish. Then he fixed the rough edges and started painting the boats. The new color was to be YELLOW. Yes! The same color as the line down the middle of the highway. He painted the top of the boat orange. I have to admit one thing. The boat was easy to spot.

My mother was killed in an automobile accident on November 11, 1956. I was five at the time. She was buried two days later on November 13, my birthday. My father, mother, me, and a friend were taking some clothes to a needy family when we had the wreck. Its something you don't forget. Our car was hit by a drunk driver traveling at a very high rate of speed. The impact spun us around like a top. My mother was thrown from the car and came to rest about seventy-five feet from the car.

Before leaving the car she screamed "Sherman." That was the last words I ever heard her say. The wreck happened in Reidsville, Georgia.

At that time, there were no real hospitals built in the area. There was no ambulance to rush her to the hospital to be saved. A very nice gentleman, in a station wagon, stopped and picked us up and took us to the nearest doctor's office. My mother laid in the back of the station wagon bleeding to death. Everyone did all they could to make her comfortable. That night was very long and everyone was very sad. My father took me in to see my mother for the last time. We lost more than my mother that day. She was three months pregnant when she died.

I always had the greatest birthday parties. My mother would invite all my friends and we would dress up like cowboys and Indians. There was always cake and ice cream and lots of games. It was always so much fun. On my sixth birthday there were no cowboys and Indians. Only lots of sad people around. I tried to understand what had happened. I remember very little of my early years. I guess you only remember what you want to.

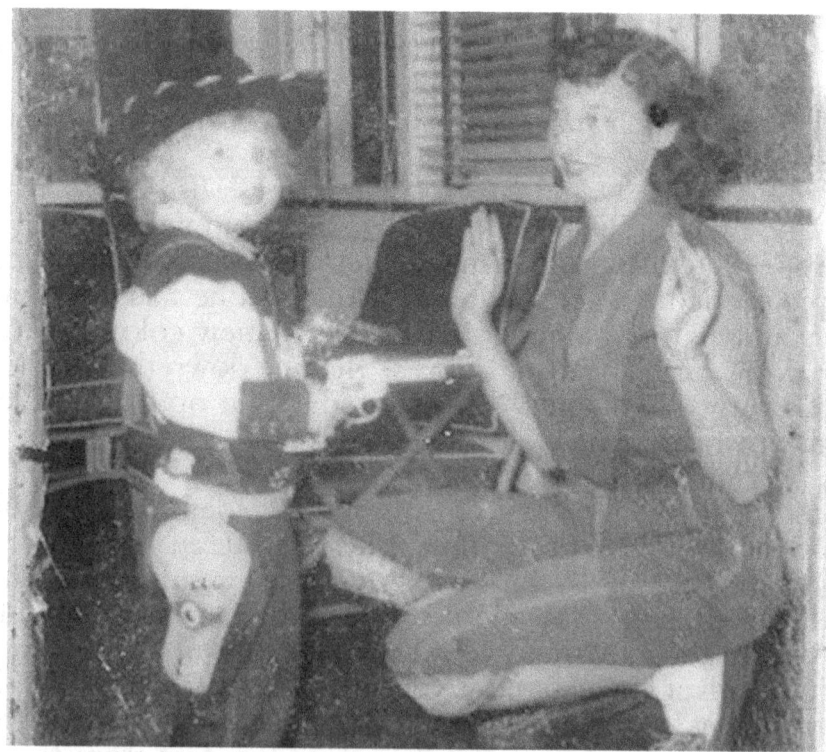

Captain cowgirl Judy, with her mother, Jerry.

After my mother's death, things were pretty much different. My father was trying to adjust and I was trying to understand why my mother wasn't around for me. I needed her so much! We must have been real close. She must have been a great mom and friend. I had an empty feeling when she died. I have a few photos of us together having a great time.

As soon as the funeral was over, my father and I went to Florida. We did not pack. We just left to go south for awhile. When we got there, we bought new clothes that we needed for the trip. I had almost grown out of everything before we returned home.

Now my father had two jobs. He had to be a mother and a father all at once. It had to be hard. I was just starting school and there was so much to do. He managed to pull it off well. He hired several housekeepers to take care of me but they seem to last only a short while.

I guess the first year was the worst year after my mother's death. There was always someone trying to take me from my father. My school principal was one of the main reasons for all these organizations trying to put me in foster homes. I believe, to this day, that her motives were not as they seem. I think she was having a secret affair with my father and she wanted me out of the way. I can't say whether she was right or wrong but I did know one thing. I had already lost one parent and I sure wasn't going to lose another. I was very young and didn't know the true facts. However, I know I didn't dream all this up. It was a real mess! We had people coming in and out of our house asking questions and taking pictures. Finally, for some reason, all this stopped as quick as it started. It was certainly was not fun while it lasted.

My father hired lots of live in housekeepers. They never seem to stay very long, although a few did and I loved them very much. They were nice company and they took good care of me. Daddy wasn't home very much at night. He was out playing the field.

We still had the charter boat business and the bait business. On weekends, I would go with my father and his fishing parties. I loved to drive the boat. He and his yellow boat were doing quite well. It was a long ride from our dock at Wilmington

Little Miss Captain Judy.

Island to the ocean. We moved the "Miss Jerry" to Captain Charlie Walsh's dock on the Lazaretto Creek, Tybee Island. Captain Charlie Walsh's (1908-1996) dock was at the mouth of the ocean with easy access to the famous "Blackfish" banks. The speed of our boat was ten knots. It took awhile to get anywhere.

My father was definitely a ladies man. He loved dating and playing the field. I believe that's what he called it. When I turned age ten, my father got married again. This would be number three marriage. Ann was a truly wonderful person and I loved her so very much. It was nice having a mother again. She also had a daughter named Annell. (I still love Ann and Annell very much. They are a very important part of my life.) It had been five years since my mother had died. They were together for a few years and then got divorced. They didn't get it right the first time so they tried again. This was my father's fourth marriage. I wonder, to this day, if she did it for another reason. I guess I wanted

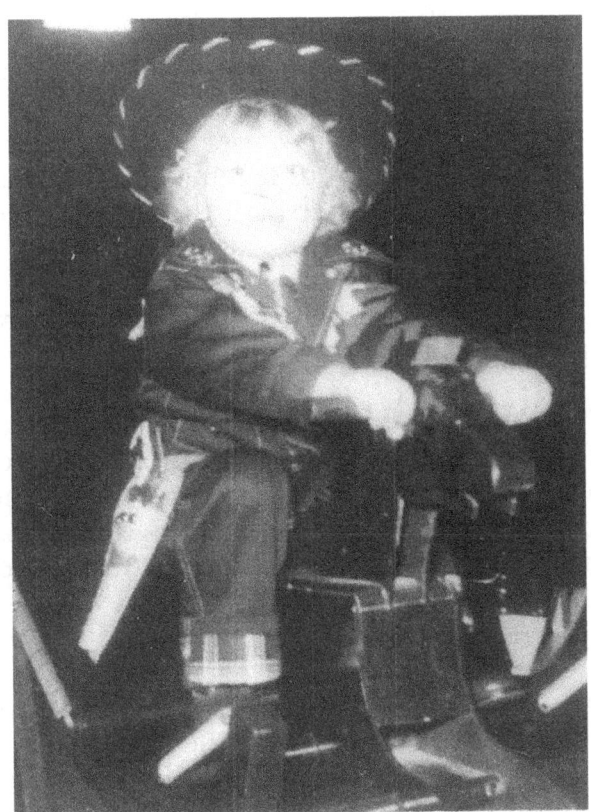

Wooden horses instead of boats.

to think it might have been because of me. It still didn't work. Divorced again! My father had been married four times by the time I was thirteen years old.

From the age of six, I had a boat. My first boats were wooden rowboats powered with three horse outboard engines. I used to think I was flying in my boat. I graduated to larger boats and motors as time went on.

As I mentioned before, I started fishing with my father on his charters when I was six years old. His boat, the "Miss Jerry" had lots of places for six year old me to play. I had my own spots. He didn't want to leave me with anyone. He hadn't decided just how he was going to take care of me, so he took me everywhere with him.

My most favorite fun was catching fish out of the starboard window located behind daddy's helm chair. The fish always seem to be biting there. While we were bottom fishing, I always seem to catch the most. When we would troll, I caught the fish right out from under the boat. They always seem to be right as the stern of the boat. You know, where the bubbles come up.

In the mornings, when we were leaving to go on a charter, I would always pick out which person I thought was going to get SEA SICK.

My favorite saying was, "Daddy that man looks very green!" I can still picture my father laughing now.

I continued fishing with him on the weekends and going to school during the weekdays. It was a great life! I could hold a compass course at the age of seven. He would let me drive home and I would even get to talk on the radio. It was so much fun. I loved the summer because I knew I would be out there on the weekends helping him run his boat. It was just fantastic! I would always pretend to be the captain, just like my father.

My father always had more than one boat. We kept the boat he used for charter at the beach. The other boats, he would buy to fix up, we kept them at home. We had shrimp boats, cruise boats, speed boats, and, of course, always lots of wooden row-boats. All our boats had a name; that name being "JUDY."

Not only did we have boats named "JUDY," we even had dogs names Judy. Daddy would be hollering for the dog and I would think he was hollering for me. The dogs and I stayed confused. Over the year we had about ten dogs named Judy.

There was one boat we had with a different name. It was called "THE BLUE BEEP." It was suppose to be a shrimp boat of sorts. We didn't have it long. We took the boat out a few times, but we had one problem after another. My father said, "It's nothing but a bunch of trouble." So we sold our problems to someone else. That's what he got for naming it something be-sides "JUDY!"

My father loved buying old broken down boats and repairing them for resale. The most boats we ever owned at one time were eight. I didn't mind having eight boats until it would start raining. Try pumping out that many boats. You might as well start pumping the first one when you finish the last.

When I wasn't fishing with my father or going to school, you could be sure I would be in my boat. I had the greatest times in my little row boats. I would get my friends together and off we would go to check out some deserted island. There was always a good time to be had. We loved to go to "Mud Puppy Creek." This was very close to my house. It's a small creek full of shrimp, crab, mullet, and lots of mud mounds. We would slide down them and splash into the water. We would even run our boats fast towards the mounds, cut them off, and go sliding across the mud. It was too much fun!

One day, we were swimming off the dock and decided to swim across the river and play in the mud. We decided to bury ourselves in the mud and wait for a boat to come by and jump up and scare them to death. We did. And, yes… We got in all kinds of trouble. We looked pretty terrible. I think I had mud in my ears for over a week.

I started water skiing when I was about ten. I loved this sport. We would ski all day long. I had my skiing partners, Johnny Sasser and Bob Turner. They were the best skiers in the area. We were all about the same age. We were very lucky that our parents kept us in boats because we sure wore them out quick. We practiced a lot together. We barefooted, skied backwards, and I even

Miss Judy sunning in her pool.

17

rode on top of Johnny's shoulders. We would have ski fights. This was accomplished by trying to put your opponent down by spraying them the most and knocking them out of their skis. We practiced on each other, but with our other opponents, we were serious. We ruled the river, that's for sure.

On my fifteenth birthday, I received the boat of my dreams. My ski boat! It was a brand new outboard with a forty-five horse power engine. It even had a racing stripe on it. At the age of fifteen, this was very important. I named my new boat "SKI QUEEN." I had a contract with Chrysler Motor Company to supply me with engines or at least keep them running so I could practice every day. I decided I was going to be a professional skier. I thought I had what it took to take the plunge. So I did. I skied in a few tournaments. It was great fun! I was a strong skier and, at least, the option was open to me to become a professional skier.

My father and I discussed this. I was just about to go into professional training when it happened... All this time, I was still fishing with daddy. He had several big boats that I would take out. What I forgot to tell you is, I wasn't supposed to take these boats out, only mine. It sure came in handy though, I got the experience I needed with the larger boats.

One day, a group of soldiers wanted to charter with my father to go fishing. They had too many people. My father suggested I might take them in his 24' Cornet. This happened to be one of the boats I was real familiar with. They did, I did, and we did. And you know what happened. The skiing became something I still loved to do. However, fishing certainly had taken first place. One trip led to another. I even got to run my father's boat. I loved his boat. It had so much room. I always felt so special at the helm of his great boat!

I don't think I mentioned it, my father met and married number five. I can't really say too much about her, good or bad. She wasn't around very long and neither was he. I don't know what the purpose was yet. Anyway, they married and she moved in with her ideas, but that didn't last very long. Have you ever heard of a six week marriage? Well, I have and daddy did. Once again, he was in the divorce court. I knew better than to get to know number five because I had figured out this marriage couldn't last long. My father was still paying alimony to number one. I think she's the one that deserved it most.

When I started running charters, I wasn't old enough to get my license. I had to be eighteen to apply. I was known as the "IL-LEGAL CAPTAIN." My file was already extremely thick. The coast guard didn't stop me from running, but they did check me out quite often. I guess they wanted to make sure I wasn't doing anything wrong. I was also driving a car before I was sixteen, so all this seem to be normal as far as I was concerned. I had to get to the boat somehow.

My father was married two more times before I turned eighteen. Number six to a woman that was half his age which only lasted a few months. I think the courting and divorce procedures lasted longer than the marriage itself. That was par for my father and his wives.

I know you're not going to believe this one! Number seven and the last one, THANK GOD, was the one of all times. She could spit fire and run a lot faster than my father could. He wasn't with her very long either. She, however, did make him decide that maybe married life wasn't for him. I was very happy when he said, "I will never marry again." I really didn't know whether to believe him or not.

After my father's failing seventh marriage, I was hoping that it would be his last. We were still paying alimony to the first marriage. I wasn't sure about the others. I did know for sure that the money was running out fast. I also learned that marriages and divorces are quite expensive.

At the age of eighteen, I was ready to take my captain's exam. This test will make you realize how little you know about how the government wants you to answer the questions. Well, I must admit, it took me several tries to pass the test. I couldn't believe the questions they were asking me. I ended up taking an oral test. Believe me, I could captain a boat, but running this piece of paper around wasn't that easy. I finally passed, took the oath, and became Captain Judy Helmey.

Straight into business I went with my father. All of his boats were named "Miss Jerry" after my mother and all of my boats were

Captain Judy Secures the Miss Jerry.

named "Miss Judy." It was an outstanding father and daughter business. Our business name was "CAPTAIN HELMEY'S CHARTER BOAT COMPANY."

My first real charter boat was a thirty footer. A wooden Chris Craft, unbelievably different from what we operate today. I had other boats but this was a qualified charter boat. "Old and ugly," as my father use to say. I didn't think so myself. I thought she was beautiful. After all, she did float! She only took on small amounts of water through her seams. But when it was rough, she did take on lots of water. All that beating and pounding seem to shift things around.

She had character and I knew she had many stories to tell if she could talk. She had a galley, a dinette, and a couch. The couch was super. The back could be lifted and it became bunk beds. The "Miss Judy" came complete with her own classic radio. The kind with tubes. My father and I would only turn our radio on at certain times of the day. He would always tell me that I might burn the tubes up if I left it on too long. One day, I turned my radio on and there was this popping noise and smoke came rushing out. I knew that it had gone to its grave. No. It was just another poor dirt dauber touching the wrong wires.

The "Miss Judy" was powered by a Gray Marine six cylinder. A gas engine that would push her about ten knots. If you pushed the throttle up a bit you might get twelve knots out of her. My father taught me how to work on that dirty old engine. I have to admit, it was fun. He bought a spare engine just in case I had a major unfixable catastrophe. When the engine arrived, I couldn't believe my eyes. It was an old engine that had been removed from an amphibious vehicle. It had an exhaust pipe that extended up about ten feet into the air. I couldn't help but wonder if my father would try to put it in with that pipe connected. He had me going for a while. He had me believing that it had to be installed that way.

The "Miss Judy" had two fighting chairs. Not like you are thinking either! My father went to the junk yard and got two matching bucket seats and mounted them on brackets. This was my fighting chairs. Oh, the helm chair was also a bucket seat. It didn't match, but it was comfortable. I always painted my boats white and, it was a known fact, daddy always painted his boats yellow. He got a deal on some paint that the highway department wanted to get rid of. Yes, he bought lots of it! He tried to get me to paint my boat yellow, but I never did. I'm glad too. I might still be doing it today.

Captain Judy waiting for her fishing party.

21

I was eighteen and just out of high school with my captain's license. My father wanted me to go to a business college so that I would have something to fall back on just in case the fish stopped biting. Or I should say, "The customers stopped biting!" I attended Draughon's Business School and received an executive secretarial diploma. While I was attending school I was fishing with my father every chance I got and taking out my own fishing parties when I was requested.

Between high school and business, I got married. I won't say too much about this because my other half turned out not to like the water as much as I did. I guess you could say it just didn't work out. We were married three years and then divorced. No children and not many things to split up.

After getting my diploma, I went to work a few places as a secretary and soon decided that getting coffee for the boss was not what I had been trained to do. I, also, was not going to do it. Boy have things changed. I think everyone gets their own coffee now.

I lucked up and landed a job with a real estate company, The Denny Company. Jimmy Denny owned and operated the business. I didn't have time to get coffee. We were too busy writing contracts. This made me think twice. Why not get my real estate license? I talked it over with Mr. Denny and he was all for it. I started studying for something that would change my whole life. It would get me involved with all the right people and into the right places. I got my real estate license and joined the ranks of the many who would try to make their fortune. I didn't make a million or even close, but what I did do is meet people. They loved to fish, so I took them. I had a brief encounter with my own real estate company, but that only lasted a while. Too much money going out and not enough coming in.

So far, my father hadn't remarried. THANK GOODNESS! He was still playing with wrecked cars. He had met up with Clem Burnsed and they had some kind of business deal. Clem had a wrecked car repair shop on the west side of town. They became good friends. They fixed up wrecked cars and fished together often. My father was happy once again. He was doing something that reminded him of his wonderful past. I am sure that Clem was learning about all those fast deals he use to make.

From the time I can remember, my father always had some-thing to do with rebuilding wrecked cars. At fifteen, I had a very special car. My first car was a convertible and it was FIRE ENGINE RED. He had it fixed up just for me. By the time I reached my twentieth birthday, I had some ten cars. My father would buy them, fix them up, and I would sell them. I had the hottest sports cars in town!

I have to admit. I did drive without a license as I did drive a charter boat without a license. It seemed quite normal to me. I would get stopped with my learners license and it didn't even seem to matter. As soon as they saw the name, I was sent on my merry way. Things sure are different now. I wouldn't think about driving without a license this day and time!

In my mid twenties, I started a business called "HELMEY BUILDERS." Yes, I was now going to build houses. Thinking back, I really didn't know what I wanted to do. You probably didn't need me to make that statement, you probably already have.

My father was seeing a lady friend in the Hinesville area. He be-gan to notice all the building activity. There were houses being built and sold on every available piece of land. There was land waiting to be sold at the right price, so we bought some. I built houses. I bought a book that showed me in detail about the structure of a house and off I went into the building business. I was a general contractor. This venture lasted about seven years. I built over fifty houses in the Hinesville area.

My father taught me a lot. One thing he always said, "You can do anything you want to, if you try." I would build houses and he would continue playing with wrecked cars and chasing wom-en. At the age of eighty, he was still catching them.

We were both still running fishing trips, mostly on the week-ends. I still loved fishing the most. It was always so interesting and never boring to me. You always met new and different peo-ple. As the seasons flew by, we fished more and more. From one day a week to seven days a week. We made a great team. He taught me everything I needed to know. All this made it easy to run the boat, catch fish and make the customers happy.

Captain Judy Helmey of Savannah, GA stands ready on her boat for her next charter-boat fishing excursion. Judy is the youngest charter-boat captain in the USA and the only lady captain that we have heard of anywhere. (Article printed in Savannah Morning Newspaper in early seventies.)

In 1975, I received the most unbelievable Christmas present. It was a thirty foot T Craft, built especially for me. My father stayed with Mr. Thompsons (the boat builder) most of the time it was being constructed. The boat was built in Titusville, Florida. I think my father stayed in the Rocket Launch Inn most of the time. All the hotels were named space something. The Kennedy Space Center is close to there.

I loved my new boat. It was the best present I had ever received. My father had put all the special touches on it. I knew he made it perfect for me. Times were great! I had a new boat. All the other "Miss Judy's" were great too, but they weren't brand new. They were play toys next to the new "Miss Judy."

My father had already bought himself several new boats, built at T Craft. In fact, he spent a lot of time in Florida building boats in the eighties. He built his and helped build others. Mr. Thompson and my father were good friends. I think my father made a good salesman.

I can only say good things about the T Crafts. After all, I still have one and have had T Crafts since the early seventies. I probably will get a bigger boat later on, but right now it's – T Craft – for me.

During the season of 1975, I changed my part of the company to "Miss Judy Charters." Daddy still had the "Helmey Charter Boat Company." He ran his business and I handled mine. There were no disagreements of sort, it was just time.

My father is ninety years old. He fished until he was eighty-three years old. He would never have fished that long without the help of Captain Bill Marsh. I've written about the dynamical duo later in the book. My father has had a great life and is still with us today. He was diagnosed with Alzheimer's disease in 1985. He has been in a nursing home for four years. I want to share with you some of the things he has done.

Captain Judy Helmey at the helm.

As you read this, please put these things on a comical side of life. I had to start laughing because crying was not the answer.

My father had always told me that there were lots of people and music playing in his house. I never gave much attention to his visitors. I knew there wasn't any. I lived in the apartment behind his house and knew when he had visitors. When my father was put in the nursing home, I moved into his house, where I was raised. Now, I can say one thing for sure. This house is definitely full of visitors and you CAN hear music playing. I don't know where it's coming from either. I have seen my mother a few times and so have some of my guests. She occasionally moves things around but I find them later. Of course, at her convenience!

When the doctor advised me that my father shouldn't be driving, I knew he wasn't going to buy that. I prolonged it as long as possible. If you were ever driving down Wilmington Island Road and there was a long line of cars, you could be sure that my father was the slow leader. I took the coil wire off and put it in my sea bag. I went fishing. Daddy also went out that day. He fixed his problem and off he went to the beach. He liked to watch the girls in their bathing suits.

I took his keys hoping that he would think he had lost them. I went fishing. No problem. He had already fixed the car so it didn't need a key to start it. Back to the beach. I came home one day and he had run over the highway signs. You know the ones with the blinking lights on them. The ones that say, "BEWARE – BEWARE." How do I know he ran them over? They were still hung under his car and some were still blinking. God only knows how long he drug them!

His ability to pick up women and secure cars did not stop when he moved to the nursing home. He had lots of the women smoking his cigars and holding his hand. He was even involved in stealing a car. Mr. Rushing, an ex-bus driver and a buddy to my father, both decided to take a ride. Someone had left their keys in the car and, of course, they noticed. In the car they went. Mr. Rushing and daddy going down the highway at a high rate of speed (about ten miles per hour). The chase was on! The nursing home finally caught up with them about five miles down the road. No one was hurt and the car wasn't damaged.

Captain Judy holding a grouper caught at the Savannah Snapper Banks.

When they got them out of the car, daddy was accusing Mr. Rushing of trying to kill him. I guess he didn't like Mr. Rushing's driving…

I visit my father as often as I can. Sometimes he knows me and sometimes he is too busy going over things in his head. I would like to think he is still fishing and fixing up those wrecked cars!

There have been many good times and may bad times, as with any kind of life or business.

I am now forty years old. I still have a hard time saying that word – FORTY. I never thought I would ever get any older than twenty. I guess it happens to everybody.

I have had a wonderful life and am still having it as we speak. How many people get to live their dreams every day? Well, I do!

In the following pages, I have tried to share with you in short story form all the wonderful things that have happened to me and my father.

FASCINATING STORIES MY FATHER TOLD

When I was five years old, I started fishing with my father on the weekends. We would go to the Black Fish Banks, which was located off Tybee Island about 11 miles offshore. Miss Jerry's speed was about 12 knots. That was a good speed for a boat in the late fifties. I loved going with daddy on his charters. He would tell the most fascinating stories about his past. He would always have the whole party up around his helm chair listening. Their ears all perked up, as he told them the most unbelievable stories. I would like to share those great stories he told.

One day, while offshore in the Miss Jerry, a big water spout sat down right on top of his boat. He said the water was far up as you could see. The boat was spinning like a top, as it was caught up in the circular motion of the spout. Daddy had no control of the boat as she bounced off the walls like a bullet from side to side. Fearing for sure the boat was to be lost and the people drowned, all he could do was hope for a miracle. As fast as it came, the waterspout went. Everyone on board was very scared including my father. I still wish I had been there.

Captain Helmey making his special rigs.

A freak wave hit his boat and turned her over on her port side. All the passengers in the stern of the boat were thrown out. Windows were broken and anything that wasn't tied down was flying around. The water started rushing in. Daddy knew this was the end! In an instance, another freak wave hit the boat and sat her back up right.

My father always told of his running days when he worked for Big Al. For six years, he said he built cars that Big Al used to haul rum from Wilmington Island. I think my father loved this time of life most. He always had a sparkle in his eye as he told of his travels with Big Al. he even told me, one day that him and a well known locksmith in Savannah made the deal of a life time. I don't remember what he said they did for the $200,000.00 big ones! The only problem was that it was all counterfeit... That usually put a smile on everyone's face.

My father would take divers out. I think I was about seven at the time. I remember them dressing up in those jet black rubber suits, none like the colorful ones they have today. "The frog-men," I called them. (Too much television.) They always looked so strange. My father would carry them out to the submarine.

Captain Helmey contemplating his fishing spot.

He told me it was an old German submarine he had found. The sub had met it's end in World War II. He also said he thought it was a submarine that sunk two or three shrimp boats as they were trawling in front of Tybee Island. It seems as though the submarine got hung up in the nets and turned the boats over in the shipping channel. It was never heard how the sub got sunk. All I know is that it is laying there on the bottom of the ocean floor some were very close to the Texas Tower. My father would go to it without any problem. At that time, we had no LORANS! or any other kind of direction devices. The submarine was not marked with any buoys or lights. The bow of the sub was buried in the sand. The rest had just lain atop the ocean floor.

The divers would jump off the Miss Jerry and seem to be gone forever. Daddy would always tell me that there were bodies probably still down there in some of the old compartments. I used to think, suppose they are still alive and waiting for us to rescue them. My father had told me the divers had seen a woman through one of the glass windows in the sub. it's wonderful when you are a child, you can believe anything you hear. When it came to telling stories, my dad really knew how to keep my attention…

I visit that old sub every now and then. There sure are a lot of fish hanging around it. I am sure it would be a diver's paradise but I better keep this one to myself…

My relationship with my father was more than just a daughter/father type. We were best buddies and best friends. Every Wednesday night we would go out. Well, after a hard day of fishing, why not? We would go to the famous Johnnie Harris's located on Victory Drive. My father went there a lot more than just Wednesdays. I could tell, everyone seemed to know him too well. We would always eat supper in the ball room. It was great! The ceiling looked as though it was the sky at night. It had stars and a moon. It all looked so real. In fact, I wanted to think it was. There was always a band playing. Usually Gene Taggert was there singing his songs. Daddy would ask me to dance. Of course, I would accept. Off we would go, to the dance floor. I will never forget all those different styles of shoes he would wear. I shouldn't. I use to stand on them as we floated across the dance floor. My father was an outstanding dancer!

Have you ever eaten Crow? No, I mean real crow? The feathered ones, the ones that fly. We've all have a taste of the other a few times, I'm sure.

My father enjoyed bird hunting very much. He also liked to call the birds that he was hunting. That way he didn't have to walk so far. One day, we sat down by the dock and he called the crows. Only a couple came at first. He said they had come to see if the coast was clear. Well, here we were, kind of in the bushes. Well, let me rephrase that. We were very much in the bushes. My father, with his 12 gauge and me, only eight years old. We watched as the two look out crows checked it out. Sure enough, they flew off. A short time later, here comes the whole flock, just as daddy had said. We picked them up and you guessed it, daddy cleaned them. I can't remember how. I guess I never need to know, since I don't plan on serving them to my future guests.

My father fired up the old grill that he had made out of old car parts. We put the crows on and barbecued them. All I can say is that we ate them I don't remember if I liked them or not, but I do know one thing for sure, everyone else must have. There were no left overs!

There was the mermaid that daddy would always catch. I still remember the way he described her. She had long blonde hair draping over her body that covered her breast and back. She was half woman and half fish. (Of course.) Her tail was long and covered with large scales. He said she would beg and cry for him to let her go. Of course, he did. She is still out there. I see her every day!

One day, my father was fishing about 11 miles offshore. He said it wasn't very rough, the sun was shining, it was just a wonderful day. They had been doing some bottom fishing for black sea bass, they were catching a few. The king mackerel had made their appearance. They were darting at the black fish as the people were trying to get them aboard. A few times they would pull in half a fish. I guess you could say, they were sharing their catch with the kings.

Daddy kept seeing a shiny object off in the distance. He kept watching it on and off. It appeared to be getting closer each time. It finally got the best of him. He told the fishermen to pull their lines in. He had to take a look at this shiny thing.

As they approached this floating object, it began to move toward the boat. As it moved, he said he was very shocked to see that it was a very large rattle snake! Oh, by the way, my father is very scared of snakes. He says they make him hurt himself. My father immediately pulled away to figure out what to do. They decided to bring this sea serpent aboard. Daddy was going to attempt to kill it and put it in the boat. At least that was how it was suppose to be. The snake had to be real tired, but he must have had some energy stored up for his leap to what he thought was dry land. They were trying to kill the snake, but somehow the snake got into the boat ALIVE...

My father said there was a panic in every direction! Everyone wanted up and the snake wanted down. Daddy finally killed the snake with an oar. He tied a string around his or her neck. He said he wasn't sure if there were any riders inside. I'm sure he didn't want to find out.

My father brought the snake home in a five gallon bucket. It almost filled the bucket up. Well, I bet you're wondering what we did with it. What else? We put it in the bushes and called our next door neighbor, Mr. Bridges. Daddy told him to come over, we had something he wanted to show him. When he walked by the bushes we hollered, SNAKE! I never knew Mr. Bridges could have been a perfect candidate for the high jump...

Captain Helmey after a hard day of fishing.

As I ride in the coastal waterway, I can't help but think of all the interesting tales the rivers and creeks could tell you if they could talk. My father use to take his 40 foot yacht, the "Miss Jerry," (named after my mother) off for weeks.

They would go to Florida for a few months then head back home for the summer. That was long before me and the charter boat business. Before all of the travels to Florida, he traveled the creeks and rivers in search of other things besides fish and shrimp.

It was never proven for sure, of course, but rumor has it that there was a little smuggling going on in this area. When daddy and I would go fishing, he would always say, "See that spot, the spot with the old broken off piling, we use to pick up our cargo there." He would always say, "We never really found it all, some cases must have sank deep into the soft mud." Those statements made me just want to start digging until I found some proof. An old bottle maybe, with a good cork. I know I'm just dreaming, but why not, it's my paper.

I have pictured of wooden rowboats. We must have had at least twenty. (I have included a picture.) At the age of five, we still had rowboats. I never, to this day, have had anyone say to me, "I remember your father use to rent my family a rowboat now and then." Who knows? He might have. Although I can't find any proof. What else would you do with twenty rowboats but rent them?

Captain Helmey and his many rowboats.

Captain Judy does a radio check.

POWERS THAT BE

My father had a few run ins with the electric company. It seems as though they wouldn't give him a contract for what they were going to charge him. Things still haven't changed too much, we are still dealing with the powers that serve us. You have to pay what they say or lose it. Very simple, right? The electric company came by to deliver his bill. He looked at it and said, "I am not going to pay this bill." Of course, you have to pay it, or you guessed it, your power will be cut off. Daddy gave them an answer they were not use to hearing, "Cut the lights off!" At this point, they knew or thought they knew he could not run a business without electricity.

They watched him of course. Well, he could operate a business without their electricity… He did not need theirs, he had his own. That night the electric company drove by and saw lights coming from HELMEY'S GARAGE. They knew he had tied into their power and they thought they had him this time. The next morning, the officials visited him. Knowing they would be there, he was ready. They wanted to check everything. My father told them to get their poles and get off his property. Of course, they laughed and so did he. He smiled and said, "I'm going to give lights to the whole block for free," and "I'm going to show every business owner how they can get power cheaper with no hassles."

My father had bought a large diesel generator. He built a room by code for it. At the flip of a switch, he could change from the electric company over to his. Oh, by the way, the generator was low maintained and fuel cost was very low. Daddy had extra parts and the knowledge to fix it, if it broke. He was set. While he was explaining what was going on, the officials kept saying, "You can't do this," and my father would reply, "I already have!"

In the end, the power company gave him a contract. They didn't move their poles and he didn't move his generator.

I remember another run in my father had with the "powers" that be. I came home one day from fishing and found a policeman standing in the yard. Well, that was not unusual, they always came by to check on the place and to talk to daddy. Unfortunately, this was not the case. He was here on a complaint.

It seems as though my father had forgot to pay his electric bill. An employee had come by to cut off his electricity. (Now remember, my father is over 80 years old at this point.) The gentleman explains to him the problem and what he has to do. He gets up, starts to walk off and the gentleman asks, "Captain Helmey, are you going to get me a check?" "No," he replied, "I am going to get my gun!"

Now you know why the policeman was there. At any rate, he didn't turn his lights off. He was in quite a hurry when he left! Yes, we paid the bill and no, we didn't have a spare generator with a dual switch. I wish we did, I might be using it now.

Captain Helmey and his favorite dog, Judy.

FULL MOON ADVENTURES

My father was a great shot, I could never figure out how he could shoot with the old shot gun, but he did. His gun was a very old automatic twelve gauge. I remember the stock was held together with electrical tape. I believe, to this day, that the barrel was even a little crooked. I couldn't hit anything with it myself. You have to realize, at the age of ten, I was busy just picking myself up after the blast. I kept trying.

We would load up the old boat with all the essential gear. Life preservers and oars. You know who had to use the oars, me, they fit my hands perfectly. The rest of the stuff was the cannon, shells and a dip net. The net fit my hands too! We had to pick the birds up, right? Daddy and I would take off. If you hadn't already guessed, we were going marsh hen hunting. We did most of our hunting across from the Savannah Inn. We would go early in the mornings as the water was rising to a spring tide. "Full moon," my father would say.

I would row, he would shoot, and I, of course, would dip, I guess, by now, you can figure out who did most of the work and who had most of the fun. I still had a great time. Work or not, it was just great fun. I still, to this day, can see us heading out on our hunt.

When we had shot our limit, we would head home. The best part was yet to come. Now someone had to clean these birds and you are wrong, no, I didn't have to do it. Thank God! My father would skin them and I would help cook them. He would first cover them in flour and then deep fry them. Boy, the kitchen sure was a mess, flour everywhere. Then he would make a gravy with catsup. The best stuff in the world. He would put the gravy into a big pot along with the fried marsh hens and cook them some more. They were delicious! I mean think of all the time it took to prepare them, your bound to be hungry when you finish.

I remember one time my father and a good friend of his, Remer, went off to get their limit of hens. Daddy had his usual things but Remer had a little more. He had his cameras and his hunting equipment. Off they went. Remer was going to take my place and row until my father got his limit and then I guess he was going to row until he got his limit. My father never really learned how to row, at least he told all of us that…

As they moved across the Wilmington River, the small boat was overtaken by a wave and the boat capsized. It was very cold. Into the water they went. They floated up the river to the first dock and they climbed up.

Remer said he was worried about my daddy but as it turned out, my father floated like a cork. He could float shoulders high without moving his feet or hands. It was amazing! I use to dive down to watch to make sure he wasn't bluffing me.

When the boat capsized, Remer lost all his cameras, his gun and my father, of course, lost his old faithful gun too.

The new gun he bought never exactly came up to par. It didn't have any character and hadn't been in as many places. Daddy was still a great shot, although, we didn't have any marsh hens for supper that night…

Captain Sherman Helmey taking a break on the Miss Judy Too.

JUNK YARD MONKEY

When I was eight, my father showed an interest in an auto repair shop. I believe the name of the place was Simple Simon's Auto Repair. (I am not sure.) I use to go there all the time with him. There was always a lot of wrecked cars, they were repairing. I use to fall in deep thoughts about each car wondering if anyone had been hurt or even killed in them. Out back was a graveyard of old discarded wrecked cars. The ones that didn't make the repair were used for spare parts. I use to go out back and gaze at all of them. They was always a junk yard dog to play with. Their names always being Bumper, Crash, or just plain old "Ugly."

Then there was the cage that was next to the building out back. Daddy used to always say, "Judy don't go out there by that cage because the monkey in that cage is real mean. Stay away!!" Well, I was eight and the monkey was locked in the cage. Of course, I wasn't going in that stupid cage, but I was going out there to see the monkey. I slowly strolled over to the cage. After all, I had to watch out for that mean monkey in the cage and my father.

When I got to the cage, there he was, that monkey didn't look so mean. So I walked around to the front of the cage. He still just sat there and watched me as I watched him. He didn't move, except for his little hand. He moved it under his little bottom. It looked as though he was sitting on it. He wasn't. He threw the contents in his hand at me. Boy, what a mess. The smell was terrible!! How had so little covered so much? Well, as you can guess, he wasn't sitting on his little hand. It goes without saying, I didn't have to tell daddy what I had been doing. I was just glad he didn't make me ride home in the trunk...

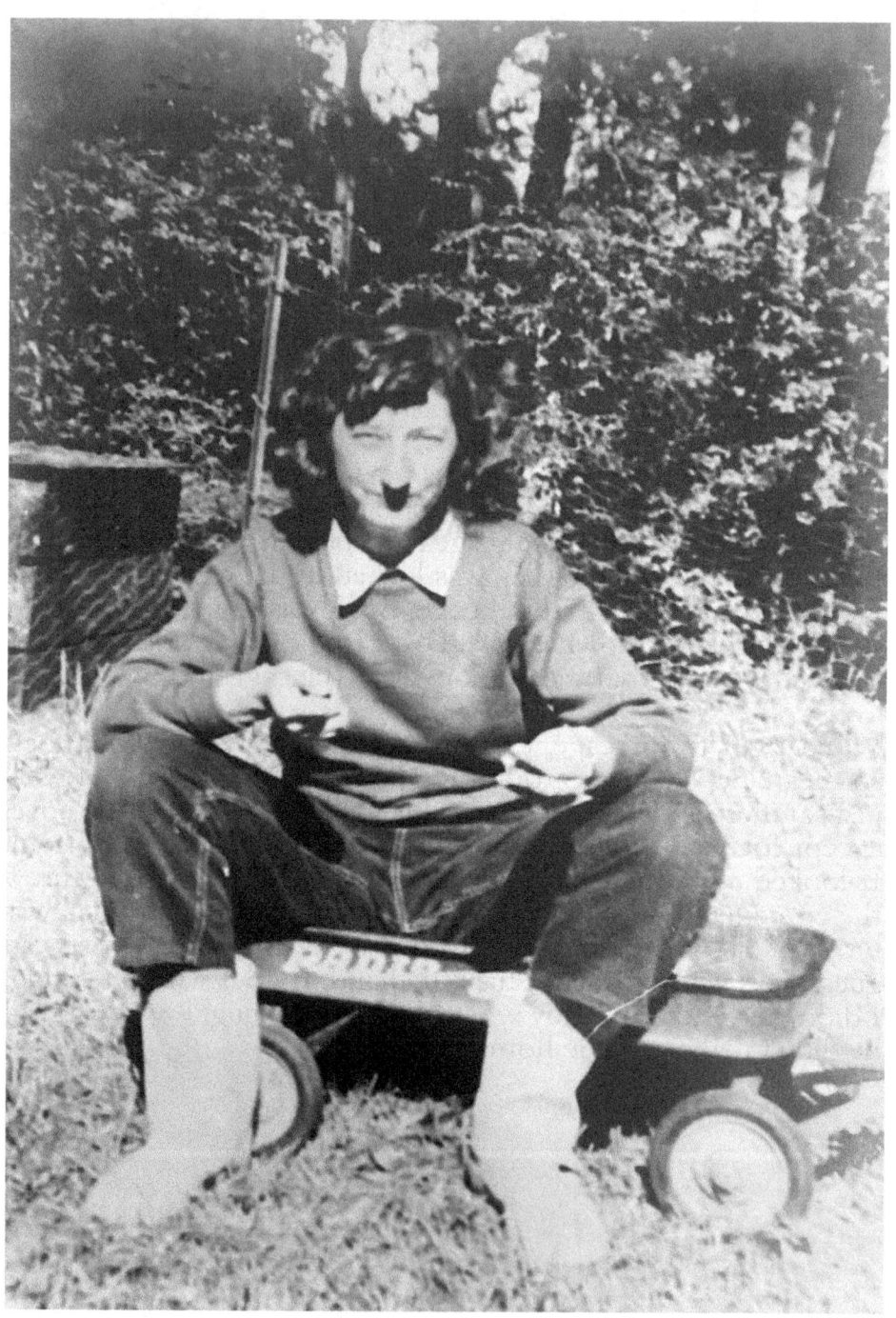

My mother, Jerry Helmey.

RATTLESNAKES AND RABBITS

In the middle sixties, we had our boats docked at Captain Walsh's dock, located at Savannah Beach. Each morning of our fishing trip, we rose early, got our wash tub and filled it with ice from our ice machine. Then we would be off to Woo's Seven-Eleven to wait for their seven o'clock opening of the store. You could set your clock by Soc (the owner). Soc would soon arrive; we would go inside and have our usual. Daddy would get a quart of milk and I could get a coke, bag of corn chips, and, of course, some bean dip. Healthy breakfast! At least it wasn't sardines, they were for lunch.

After our short morning conversation, we were off to the beach. The ride lasted about fifteen minutes. There were always rabbits sitting on the roadside. For as long as I can remember, we always played a game on our journey. Whoever had the most rabbits, or cows on his or her side of the road won. I would always have to fudge a little because I thought daddy was too. There was at least thirty to forty rabbits every morning. He would always say there are lots of big rattlesnakes in the marsh. Where there are rabbits you will find lots of snakes. Snakes have them on their diet, I guess. After turning off to go to the boat, we had a long narrow road with more rabbits. When we got out of the car, I would always look for those snakes.

My father and I would take the ice down to the boat. We would dump it into our fish boxes. I usually brought the tub back to the car and put it in the trunk. One morning, he must have been feeling a little chipper, he jumped off the boat and took it himself. He was holding the tub with one hand and it was kind of swinging back and forth. When he reached the end of the dock, I heard a loud noise. It sounded as if someone had thrown an orange at the tub. I looked up at my father, he was moving rather briskly. He began hollering, "Stay down there." Well, of course you know what that means, come here and look. I could tell he was busy doing something. As I got closer, I could see he had a stick and was trying to pick up something. It was one of those giant rattlesnakes. The snake had struck at the tub, I guess because it was shinning in his face. He hit the tub so hard and direct that he knocked himself out or had killed himself. It didn't matter to me which he had done because, as far as I'm concerned, there are only two kinds of snakes. I don't like a live or dead one. Daddy disposed of the snake. He probably put it in the bushes so Captain Walsh would get the living daylights scared out of him.

Captain Helmey and his daughter, Captain Judy. What a team!

DEAD BODIES

My father's encounter with dead bodies didn't occur very often, but it was something that he never seem to forget.

He found a body floating outside the north end of the jetties. He followed correct procedures. He called the coast guard and they rushed over to his location.

Upon arrival, my father showed them what he had found. He waited to see how they were going to retrieve the body. Staying to watch was a big mistake! The coast guard lowered a basket and with the assistance of their dive team, they shifted the basket under the floating body. As they lifted the basket up, a horrible thing happen. The skin and flesh just poured off this body flowing out through the basket. My father said it was the most horrible thing he had ever seen.

His second and last body was found in the Savannah River area. He tied the body to a buoy and called the coast guard. As soon as they arrived, he departed.

My closest encounter with a so called "body" was a hog that had been bitten in half by something. Who knows what? It looked like it might have been something else, so I called the boat behind me which happen to be Steve Amick, owner and captain of Neva Miss Seven, and let him do the looking. I decided to take my father's word on how these things affect you....

Captain Judy Helmey.

MULLET JUMPING

My father introduced me to many different kinds of water spots. Have you ever been "Mullet Jumping?" Well, if you haven't, before you leave this old' world, you need to try it at least once. It's a real blast! When my father and I would go, we would always come back with lots of mullet. We would go up into Mud Puppy (a small creek off Turner's creek) at low tide and, of course, at night. The best time to go is on a full moon. All you have to do is get in the area where the fish are schooling and turn the old spot light on and they jump in the boat. I have tried many ways to protect myself from these leaping lizards. I have used a catcher's mask, snow skiing gargles, and big metal pots. Anything to protect your eyes. These fish are frantic acting. They jump straight for the light and into the boat. You get hit on the head, in the face, and everywhere else. If you survive the attack of the mullet, you go home, clean them (this is important), ice them down real good and fry them up for breakfast. They are delicious! They are also very good smoked.

When my friends and I would go, you would think we were marching off to WAR! I didn't have a helmet so I would take a pot, scuba mask, and a white sheet. Of course, getting ready for this ordeal is as much fun as catching the mullet. We would always look quite a sight! Some would wear football helmets and some would wear army helmets. It was a very interesting sport. The mullets were always very good to eat but the fun was getting there.

Captain Sherman Helmey.

SUMMER CAMP

I will never forget the time my father got the idea to send me to summer camp. This, I am sure, was not his idea. I had summer camp at my house every day. I had my suspicions on who might be behind all this, but I'm not sure till this day. Off to camp I went. For two weeks of fun in swimming pools and maybe a ride in a boat. You have got to be kidding! It wasn't too bad. Everyone was very nice, although, I had quite a time getting adjusted.

The first day I was there, I figured out how I might get home quick. I thought it was a great idea. I would throw all my clothes away and my father would have to come and get me. Right? Wrong! He did come, but only to bring more clothes. I knew I must have been doomed. It turned out that I did have a good time. I met a lot of new friends and spent a lot of time in the pool.

Daddy and I would go shrimping in front of Tybee Island. It was so great! I couldn't wait for him to pull the net in. there was so many kinds of fish, crabs and shrimp in it. He would dump the catch into a big box with low sides and we would sift through everything and pick out the shrimp and let the rest go. I would keep the crabs. We loved boiled crabs.

My father liked boiled shrimp the best. He never bothered to take the shell off. He just put the whole shrimp in his mouth and chewed it up and down the hatch it went. We had a friend who showed him how to fix the shrimp so that the shell would be soft and almost become part of the meat. It was pretty good. I don't care too much for whole shrimp, just the meat.

I will never forget the day we pulled the shrimp net in and had the biggest turtle I had ever seen. Up close that is! The turtle had gotten tangled in the net while we were dragging for shrimp. Daddy said, "Don't get close to that turtle he might bite you." I just wanted to pet him. His skin looked so rough and unusual. So dad turned around to get something and I thought I would give this turtle a poke with the scrub brush handle. I took the handle and kind of put it close to his mouth. Boy, was I shocked. He bit the end of the handle off. Now, I knew why I was supposed to stay away from him. I'm sure when daddy turned around he could tell I was in shock, however, he didn't say anything. He had been busy changing the gas tanks and letting the old turtle catch his breath. We let him go. I still don't know if he swallowed the end of the scrub brush handle or just spit it out when we turned him back to the sea.

My dad and I spent a lot of time together in the spring and summer. Besides fishing, shrimping, and crabbing, we would work on his boat. I could get places he could not fit. He was a big man. I, also, liked doing things that he must have disliked. One thing I don't think he liked very much was cleaning the bottom of the boat. Boy, was she a big one!

The "Miss Jerry" looked even bigger when you were under her looking from one end to the other. I would clean down one side and then the next. It would take me days. I never once thought "I wonder what daddy is doing up there in the boat. He is so quiet." Now that I think of it, do you think he was sleeping?

Working with wooden boats is a lot different that working with fiberglass. Wooden boats required a lot more maintenance. The wooden planks that made up the bottom of the "Miss Jerry" were forever coming loose and getting the dreaded worms in them. These worms would leave little holes behind as evidence they had been there. Daddy would check the bottom and looks for soft places and holes. If we found a real bad plank, we would replace it. He would replace the plank and take this cotton looking material and stuff it in the cracks between the planks. He used this caulking compound afterward to hold the cotton in. Let me tell you, if you get the cotton and the caulking compound on your hands and it dries before you can get it off, you have big problems. Your fingers stick together so much that if you try to pull them apart, it feels like your skin is going to come off. While it is wet, of course, you have to get it in your hair, ears, and nose. This, of course, is the only time you get an itch.

After washing her down, it was time to put the paint on. The paint was very expensive and daddy would always say "Don't spill any of the paint, be extra careful." I would always spill the paint. I always seem to step where I put the paint pail down. I wonder if he ever noticed that I used more paint sometimes than others. After painting, there would be an inspection. Yes, he would come down and inspect the bottom for "Holidays."

My father's definition for this was the area that I missed or merely waved the brush over. I mean, I wasn't perfect. Anyway, it was dark under there and every now and then I might hear things moving, so I had to move faster. The "Holidays" were quickly covered by more paint. Then he would praise my work and say, "She's ready to float once again." And float she would and leak she would. Until the caulking swelled up in the cracks, she would leak like a sieve!

We would pump her dry and then we would pump her some more...

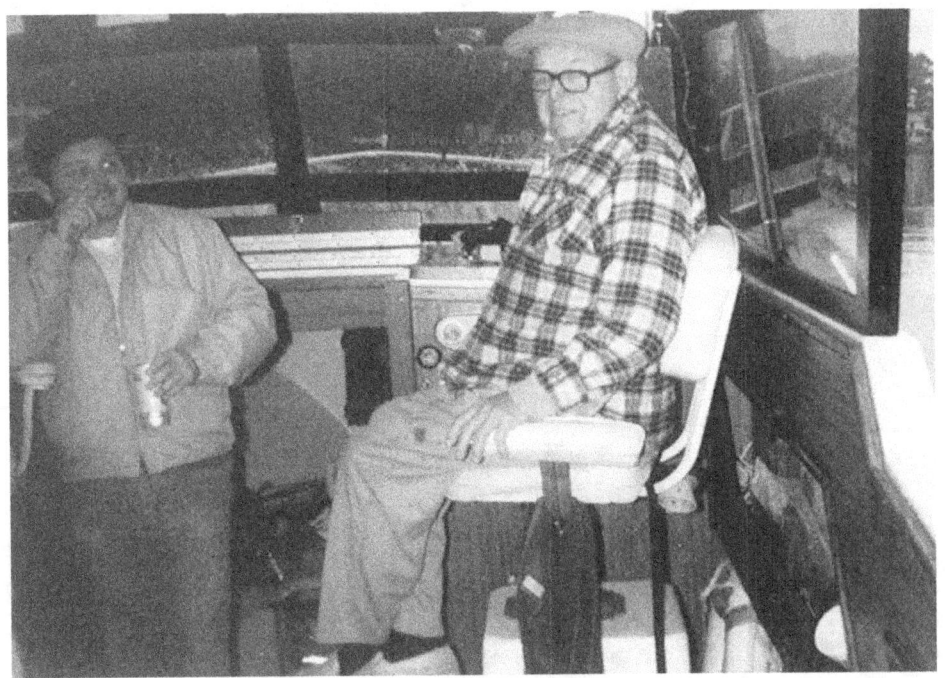

Captain Helmey and friend Captain Chuckie Fischer.

Captain Kathy Brown fighting a big one.

JUDY'S EIGHTY POUND COBIA

Out of all the fishing my father and I would do, I think he loved cobia fishing the most. We would go out to the shipping channel and fish the buoys. We would sometimes use eels or live shrimp for bait. They were both very good. I can see daddy now pulling that big forty foot boat up next to the buoy. He would run aft and throw his float out, waiting for the big one to hit.

Cobia are very curious fish. They lay under buoys, driftwood, or anything that provides shade. The feed on all the smaller fish. As soon as you pull up to the buoy, they come out and circle the boat. If you are quick and put the bait in front of the fish, sometimes he will take it right away, then there are time when they swim around the boat not wanting to smell your bait. This is when my father would move the quickest I have ever seen. He would run to the bow of boat and look for his GREAT CIS-CO KID, which by the way, is the lure of all lures. It is almost guaranteed to get the cobia's attention. Daddy would hurriedly attach the lure and start casting it out and pull it through the water to attract the uninterested fish. If that didn't work, he would pull the lure real close to the tip of the rod and jerk, slap, and pound the lure in the water. All the noise and splashing would cause the cobia to go mad. He would start darting and chasing the lure.

I don't know what part I liked best, watching that fish chase the lure or daddy's face as it would light up as he felt he had control of the crazed fish. He would make the cobia so mad; I think it would have struck anything you put in front of it. Sometimes it would even leap out of the water to get the lure. When the fish finally made contact with the bait, it usually hit so hard that it broke the cisco kid in half. Thank goodness we got the right half still tied to the line. The fish would run straight for the bottom so quick that you better not have your thumb too tight on the reel or you may be missing some skin. The fight would be on.

The cobia is a strong fighting fish. It's very hard to tire this fish out. This fish needs to be completely worn out before you attempt to gaff it and put it in the boat. They are very strong and if they hit you with their tail they could do damage to you and your boat. A thirty pounder and up is a good twenty minute fight, a full fight at that. My father called a fish that had a lot of fight left, VERY GREEN,

The fish that my father caught was in the thirty-five pound range. A very good size. We went to the next buoy to look for our next victim. Sure enough, they were there, not one but a bunch of them. They immediately came to the boat and I threw the bait at them. I was using live shrimp. Soon as the float hit the water the fish took the bait. Down the float went! I waited for my usual three or four seconds (which by the way seems to be an hour) and set the hook. At this time, I wasn't sure whether he had me or I had him. He took off as if he had a plane to catch. I started screaming for daddy to help me. He, of course, just laughed, "You caught him, you catch him." I had heard that before. Well, that was yet to be seen. I think the fish knew what was going on up in the boat. I was only eight. I was beginning to think that the fish was older and smarter than me. I was in this on my own. Daddy wasn't going to help me, but what he did do was holler a lot. "Keep your line tight. Don't give him any slack. Hold your rod up. Reel, reel, reel!" At this point, I am on the floor and the fish is very much in control. This fish had drug me across the floor more than once. I know I can't give up. I have got to get this monster to the boat somehow.

I split my pants from all that dragging across the floor that, by the way, which needed very badly sanding and painting. I wasn't going to mention, because he would probably make me do it. Finally, I could tell the fish was getting a little tired, I sure was. Daddy kept saying, "A little closer and I will be able to gaff him." Finally after another fifteen minutes, I got the fish close enough and my father brought him aboard. I was sure a tired mess and so were my pants. The cobia was much bigger than the one my father had caught earlier. I couldn't believe I had really got this one in by myself. The cobia tipped the scales over eighty pounds. No wonder I had a hard time, he weighed more than me. What a fight it had been! My arms ached and my shoulders had had enough! I was just plain tired. I guess you could say that I fished till I dropped. We ended up with four cobia that day. My father caught three fish, all under forty pounds. I guess I need to mention again, mine was over eighty pounds...

That old trick with the Cisco Kid really does work. I still use it quite often to get that cobia that doesn't seem to be interested in anything you have to offer.

Miss Judy standing by her eighty pound cobia.

Ruby Brock showing off her amberjack caught on the Miss Judy too.

Brenda Shirley proud of her large cobia after a great day of fishing.

MYSTERY SEA

When my father and I were out fishing I would see patches of yellow weed floating by. He called it sargasso weed. He said that it had drifted hundreds of miles from the Sargasso Sea. This sea is located in the northern part of the Atlantic. In the old days, ships would avoid this area of the sea. There were reported rumors of giant sea monsters and islands that would be there one minute and gone the next.

I did a little checking at the local library on the Sargasso Sea. It's very interesting how things change over the years. The more you know about the area, the less you are afraid of it.

The Sargasso Sea covers about 2,000,000 square miles. All the current around the sea moves in a clockwise motion. It is the home of some strange and different marine animals. Among one of these is the Sargasso fish. It is a strange looking fish indeed. Imagine a fish with short arms and long fingers, about ten of them. Five on each hand. They use these hands to help them attach themselves to the weed, which by the way, is their host. They live off the marine inhabitants that also make their home in the weeds.

Another interesting thing that happens in the Sargasso Sea has to do with the migration of the American and European eels. This area of the sea is their spawning grounds. The eels spend a lot of their lifetime between the fresh waters and the Sargasso Sea. At spawning time, the eels leave their freshwater and make their journey to the sea. They spawn and then they die. The young eels then return to the river about one to two years later to start the process again.

When I am out fishing at the snapper banks, we see large areas of weed. We often troll by the patches. Dolphin, king mackerel, and cobia sometimes are found laying in the shade. Also, I have seen quite a few sail fish swimming around it hoping to find a quick meal.

Ben Greene showing off his amberjack caught on the Miss Judy Too.

AMAZING DISCOVERIES OF SHARKS

The first time I ever heard about sharks was when my father would come home from fishing and tell me about them. I believe I was around the age of six. He would come home with the most fascinating stories. He would tell me how hard they would fight and how the people were always so afraid and amazed at the same time at these fish we knew so little about. My father would say, "When you catch them, fight them until they get real tired. Get the fight out of them," he would always say. He would get a long rope, attach one end to the boat and the other end he would put a slip knot and lasso the shark's tail. I never thought about how hard that must have been until I tried it myself. Can you imagine trying to lasso a 300 pound shark? A mad one at that!

Anyway, he would lasso this shark and pull it backwards until his guts would choke him or he would drown. We would cut the jaw bone out. We would take the shark eyes and boil them. If you did this, you would end up with pearl looking stones that were hard as a rock. They were great to take to school for my science project. We would take the fins and jaw, pour salt on them, and let them dry out. We tried boiling the jaw to get the excess meat out but the teeth kept falling out.

We would fry up the meat. Shark is very good if it is cooked properly. My father always had that under control. He was a great cook and I was a great helper. He would always say, "Eat what you want and we will throw the balance away." We always kept all our other fried fish, but not the shark. He showed me why. You can take a piece of well fried shark, put it in the ice box overnight, and the next morning, blood will be running out of it. I have no explanation for this happening.

When cleaning a shark you may feel the shark move or wiggle a bit. If you take the meat and lay it directly on the ice, it will sometimes move quite a bit. This may happen even if the shark has been dead for over six hours. If you don't believe me, ask Kathy Daniels about the shark meat dancing in her cooler.

We never took many pictures of the sharks my father caught but I managed to get a few with the help of my customers. I have some real fascinating experiences with sharks. My father would tell me about the fifteen to eighteen foot shark he had seen. Until I saw one for myself, I didn't know the thrill he must have experienced.

What a Catch! A 215 pound nurse shark.

KING NEPTUNE

One afternoon, when I got home from school, I decided to take my boat around to Tybee. We had our boats docked there because it was much closer to the ocean especially with boats that only ran 10 knots. You had to be close!

My father had brought it home to do some repairs and I was supposed to take it back when I had plenty of daylight. I thought to myself, it seems like a good time to go. I got everything ready and off I went. It normally took about two hours to make this trip. About half way through the trip, I realized that it would be getting dark soon. I was beginning to think that maybe I had left a little later than usual. Well, it was really getting dark and I knew it was much later than I thought.

As I got closer to the ocean, I could tell the wind was picking up. The river was getting a small chop to it. I finally got to the turn off at Lazaretto Creek. I was tired and a little scared. As I was making my turn, it left me wide open to the open seas. The waves were pounding on my port side. A big wave caught me and threw me from my seat. My heart was pounding! I knew there was shallow water to my right and open water to my left. I didn't want to go right and I certainly didn't want to go into the mud either!

As I as getting up, I looked around. There he was, Mr. King Neptune himself! He was so tall. The calves of his legs were as high as the water came. The depth of the water is twenty five feet. In his hand, he held a pitchfork with three points that was held way above his head. This vision was awesome! His beard was white. It hung way below his chin. He wore a gold crown on his head. Pretty amazing for a little girl that was scared to death!

I certainly got a good look at him. You would have too, if you had been as close as I thought I was to him. I don't know if he turned my boat around to keep it from running aground or if I was so scared, I did everything so fast just to get back in control of the boat. No matter, I did make it to the dock.

Now, I already know what you must be saying. I can't believe she's trying to get us to believe this story. All I can say in my defense is, "I believe it happened" so I wanted to share it with you. And besides, live a little with your feet off the ground! You will love it...

A nice catch for a good day of fishing.

THE CAPTAIN IS A LADY

Article written by Dean Wohlgemuth: GEORGIA GAME AND FISH COMMISSION

I was interviewed on August 12, 1970 by Dean Wohlgemuth, with the Georgia Fish and Game Commission. I was nineteen years old and hadn't been operating very long as a charter boat captain.

This is the article he wrote.

> The first time I saw her she was walking along the dock, carrying four large trolling rods and a bucket of squid. She was wearing a pair of shorts and striped tee-shirt, like girls wear when they go to the beach, but she wasn't worrying about towels and suntan lotion and where the boys were. She was thinking about ice and bait and if it was going to rain and what kind of sea she was going to have.
>
> "Judy Helmey" I asked; "Right." She answered, "Want to go fishing?" I had found an animal that shortly before I didn't know existed – a girl charter boat captain.
>
> Judy and her dad, Captain Sherman Helmey, run a charter boat service out of Savannah. She has been captain of her own boat for three years, quite a feat for any eighteen year old, male or female. Her career on the sea actually started when she was five years old, because that's when her mother died. "Daddy didn't have anywhere to leave me, so I had to go along with him. By the time I was a teenager, I had spent a lot of time on the water and I knew a lot about fishing," she said. "I thought it was a lot of fun and I still do."
>
> One day more customers showed up than Captain Helmey had room for, but none of them wanted to go anywhere else. Like the stand-in on Broadway, this was Judy's big chance. When Captain Helmey asked the men on the dock if any of them

THE CAPTAIN

JUDY

Judy Helmey Jones, captain of a deep-sea fishing boat, shows off a king mackerel.

IS A LADY

would mind fishing from a boat captained by his daughter, I'll bet every one of them volunteered. Ever since, during the spring, summer, and early fall, Judy has been plying her trade as a charter boat captain.

"Dad got to thinking about it awhile back and sort of thought I needed something more than just a high school education, so I took a secretarial course," Judy smiled from behind long blond hair that fell over her shoulders. "I enjoyed it, because the people were so nice to me, but I knew all along that I had rather be fishing."

Last year after Judy graduated from Savannah High School she got married, so her real name is not Helmey, but Jones. Judy Jones, charter boat captain. "Everybody in the fishing business still calls me Helmey, because of my dad, but I don't care," she laughed, "Helmey and Helmey, my dad and I are partners."

"What happens if the motor breaks down?" It was a stupid question, "I fix it," she said. "I've never had anything to happen that I couldn't handle, except once. That time I called my dad and he came over and helped us out."

With an attractive girl out on a big ocean alone with several men, do any special problems arise? "I've only had one guy that ever got out of line. So I gave him a little shove. He fell down in the bottom of the boat and after that he didn't bother me anymore. But I was sure glad he got out of there before dad found out about it."

While we were talking, carloads of fishermen were whizzing down US 17 on their way to Florida. Highway 17 runs along the Georgia Coast and I've heard it said that it carries the heaviest traffic load in the state. These fishermen are passing right by some of the greatest fishing on the Atlantic Seaboard, off the Georgia Coast. Hundreds of

Spanish mackerel are being caught here now, some as big as seven pounds. Not to mention, dolphin, king mackerel, snapper, bass, wahoo, sailfish, marlin, and even tarpon.

If you would like to give it a try, give Judy or her dad a call, area code 912 897-2478. Judy can't go to the Gulf Stream, because it's too far and her boat isn't that big. But she knows where the fish are and the rates are extremely reasonable. In fact, there are a number of excellent charter boats on the Georgia coast. Too bad so many people are in such a hurry to get to Florida.

THE END

A lot of things have changed since this article, time has flown by. The fishing surely isn't the same. I believe that we are now getting our share of fishermen that were going to Florida. They are stopping off here and they have given us a shot. Yes, it worked! Our phone number is still the same.

CAPTAIN ALI YOUNG (1955-2021)

Have you ever been shark surfing? Have you ever reached down and picked up a live shark out of the water as it swam by? Have you ever pushed a jumping barracuda over a little so it wouldn't come crashing into the boat? Have you ever picked up a very green king mackerel with your bare hands because the gaff broke? Have you ever tied a noose around the tail of a very mad 350 pound sand tiger shark? Have you ever had to stand on your head for three hours and bail the boat out because the pumps stopped working? Have you ever tried trolling seven lines out the back of the boat and still not get them tangled? Have you ever baited twelve hooks, cut bait, take fish off, keep two lines flat out, untangle lines, and listen to the captain run her mouth at the same time?

Yes! She does all of this and she still laughs and keeps that great smile on her face that everyone is so fond of... And yes, her name is, CAPTAIN ALI YOUNG.

First mate, Captain Ali Young.

My first mate who I hope turns out to be my last mate, so far, so good...

I'm glad lots of first mates throughout my years of fishing, but none can quite compare to Ali Young. I met Ali through a good friend. She was raised in the Savannah area. She moved after school to make her career in restaurant management which by the way, she was very good at. Ali was visiting her home for a few months when we met. As our conversation moved toward my occupation, I told her about my fishing adventures. Ali made the mistake of saying she wouldn't mind going fishing.

Well, I told her I could really use some help the next day. Ali told me she knew nothing about fishing but she would be happy to help in any way she could. At this point, she did know that boats were suppose to float, fish were suppose to swim, and I was suppose to catch them.

Well, she did go and nine years later she is still with me. Ali has this unbelievable way of turning what could be a normal day of fishing into the most memorable day. Fishing is only part of the trip and entertaining is the rest.

The first year Ali fished with me, her only nautical experience was knowing that boats were made to float. She was a very fast learner and became known as "The best known mate in the southeast." We make quite the fishing team! I wouldn't leave the dock without her...

After her second year, she had enough time to acquire acquired to take her captain's test. She was more than qualified for the job. Ali jumped in and studied her material and got her license with a flying breeze. She now has her Master Captains License.

Ali and I have become great friends. In fact, she and her mother Mrs. Zedna, are considered part of my family.

We have been through quite a lot together on the Miss Judy Too. A couple years ago, Ali spent five days in the hospital. A scorpion fish finned her. Thank goodness for all the immunity she had built up handling fish. This helped her to overcome the poison the fish had injected into her finger. We rushed her to the nearest landfall and an ambulance was waiting to rush her to

Scorpion Fish

the nearest hospital. It was a miracle the fish didn't fin in any of the customers. Ali was a real trooper. She never complained but when she told me she felt like she had been stung by a thousand wasps, I knew we had a problem.

Before I reached landfall, gangrene had set in and her heart rate was extremely high. It was the longest two hours I think I had ever spent in my life! I always kidded her, "You would do anything for a few days off." I had to clean the boat while she was laid up in a cool hospital room.

The scorpion fish is said to be one of the most toxic fish we have in this area. It's also known as a Diver's Nightmare. This fish hangs around the bottom and blends in with everything around it. You could easily mistake it for a beautiful piece of coral.

I talked to a commercial fisherman who told me he had caught one and removed it with a paper bag. He then threw the bag away. Someone picked up the bag and the poison was still strong enough to infect the open cut on the fisherman's hand. In all my years of fishing, I have only hooked four and believe me, that is four too many! Ask Ali...

Ali and I have been through so much together. For instance, the time I stabbed her hand with a filet knife. In one side and out the other period nobody could believe her hand would swell up that big. Although this time, she didn't take any time off. She went to the hospital, had her hand sewn up, and was back to work the next day. The only difference was we changed roles. She was the captain and I was the first mate. She drove one handed and I baited the hooks. I also cleaned the boat. Not as well as she did, but what the heck, I passed it anyway. I have to admit, she did find a lot of fish that day! In fact, as far as I'm concerned, she found too many...

I can tell you how to ruin a perfectly good day of fishing. Just enter a fishing tournament and, believe me, things that have never happened before will start happening!

I am a member of the Savannah Sport Fishing Club. We sponsor a king fish tournament every year and I always enter. Jackie Sommers always charters my boat and we fish like fools all day to beat the clock and to WIN! We have been very lucky and have always placed in a fairly good margin. I have to tell you about this one tournament.

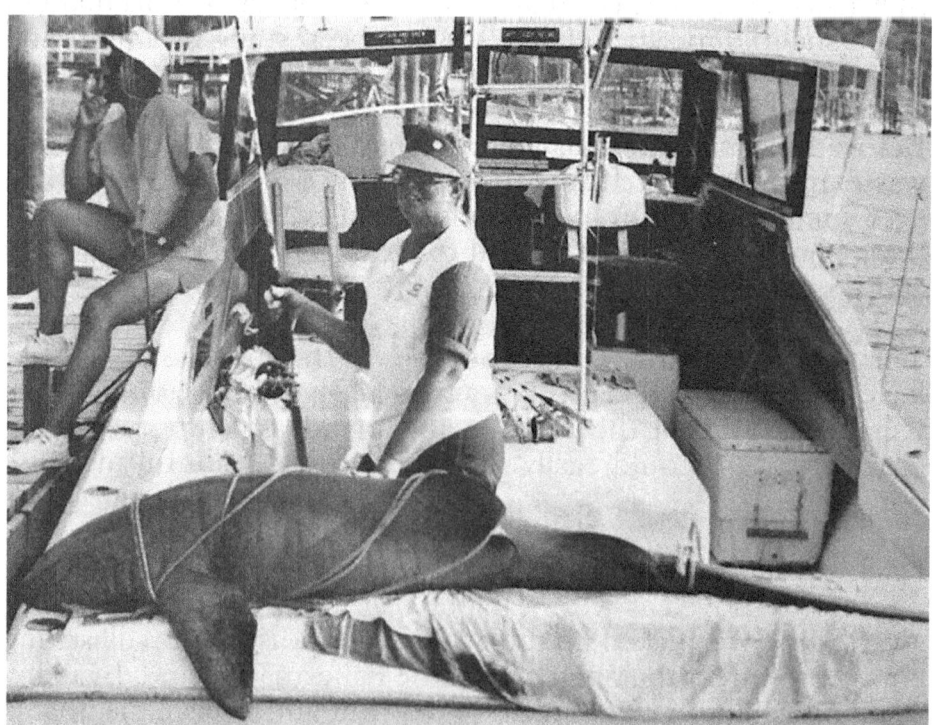

Captain Ali after a tuff wrestle with this nurse shark.

70

Jackie had chartered my boat and we were off. We were going to catch the big one! Ali had been shopping that week and had bought a lure she thought would work. I didn't say much. I just didn't figure how a white and pink hair lure was an orange head would attract many fish. I kind of figured that it might run away more than it would catch. We had planned our strategy and we were hoping that it might work at least to bring us in around 30th place. Ha! Ha!

When we arrived at our spot we started strolling. That was the plan. I don't know why. Everyone knows you catch more large kings with live fish, but anyway we had a plan. We had been trolling for about an hour and no luck. I was just about to pull in the lines and go elsewhere when it happened. We finally got a fish on, not a small fish, but a large one. Ali was busy getting the other rods in so they wouldn't get tangled up with our soon to be prize fish. Jackie had control of the fish but the fish was still very green and was still very active.

The fish was screaming through the water pitching his head trying to throw the hook. That new lure was probably making him sick at this point. I won't be laughing much longer at this lure, I promise!

First mate, Captain Ali waiting to gaff her next fish.

71

Jackie got this big king to the boat and Ali went to gaff, but the gaff handle broke off and the fish still very green, really took off! Gaff and all. He still had the hooks and, also, a trailing gaff. Normally, we would just reach for another gaff, right? Well, we would have if we had one. We both just looked at each other with blank looks. Jackie, once again, brought the fish to the boat. We looked over the side and all we could do was stare. There was our thirty pound king we had been looking for and, shortly, I was sure we would be looking for again because he was going to get away. Third time to the boat and no gaff, nothing we could use for a gaff either. The fourth time this king swam by was its last! Ali had seen enough. I screamed "No!" And she screamed "Yes!" She did exactly what I would have done, if I had enough guts. Ali leaned over and grabbing this thrashing, flapping, and jerking fish. Hooks, teeth snapping, fin jabbing, and tail flapping fish... I couldn't believe it! There she was holding this fish like it was her baby. In the boat they went. What happened after that was history had been made. We had our fish. A great thirty-two pounder. Everyone smiled. I was exhausted just from the few seconds when Ali had grabbed the fish.

We did catch one more fish that day, a little smaller than the first. Oh, and, by the way, we did borrow a gaff from Captain James Bond (1939-2010) who was fishing in our area. We only used it once that day, for the last fish.

We had only caught two fish, however, we did place and won lots of great prizes and some green stuff. By the way, yes, we did catch both fish on that orange headed lure which till this day, we haven't seen that color since. If Ali hadn't picked out the lure, we might not have caught a thing. Also, if she hadn't picked the fish up with her bare hands, we still wouldn't have had a fish. I guess you could say it was her day...

CAPTAIN BILL MARSH (1935-2013)

The first time I ever met Bill Marsh, he had chartered my boat through his company, The Hook and Line Tackle Shop. I will never forget that day as long as I live. I thought I would never meet another man that had a hair cut just like my father's. We call it the "S. I. CUT." Bill later became known as "LITTLE S.I." Yes, Mr. Bill had a genuine flat top! The finest hair cut there was, according to my father.

I have to admit, he scared me a bit, he was after one thing and was very abrupt and to the point. He wanted a big grouper, and he didn't mind fishing all day to get it either. Mr. Bill had his own rod and reel, his own fishing method which was very different from mine. He had 7/0 hooks, I thought big enough to choke the fish and 150 pound mono line for leader. An awesome rig it was!

We headed out for a full day of fishing to the Savannah snapper banks. Everyone on the boat was ready to catch anything

Captain Bill Marsh better known as "Little S.I."

that would bite their hooks, but not Mr. Bill. He had a plan. We arrived about 9:00 A.M. I started looking for some good bottom. On our first drop, we picked up an assortment of fish. We picked up blackfish, silver snapper, and vermillion snapper. The first vermillion snapper that came aboard, Mr. Bill quickly grabbed it and put it on his rig. He dropped his line as if he knew there was a big grouper down there just waiting with his mouth open. The vermillion, now called bait, was over twelve inches long.

Everyone was having a ball, catching one fish after another. Mr. Bill just stood there waiting patiently for his bite. We would move to another spot when the fishing slacked up.

Around two o'clock in the afternoon, Mr. Bill had yet to get a bite. We had to leave at three to go home. Mr. Bill still was very alert. He didn't seem to be getting bored. I saw his rod tip move a little, he stood up. He was getting a major bite. As soon as he stood up, the fish took the bait like a freight train had hit it, going over 50 mph! Mr. Bill set the hook and the rod bent over double. The tip of the rod was in the water. The fish then started pulling harder, he was trying to get back into the ledge. Mr. Bill pulled up hard and fast, reeling up the slack in the line, pulling the fish farther from his home. For the first few seconds, it wasn't clear who was in control. Mr. Bill finally got the upper hand. He started his 120 foot pull from the bottom. This fish was really pulling off drag. Mr. Bill brought the fish to the surface. We were all amazed at what we saw! I gaffed him and brought him aboard. This big lipped gag grouper had been hung before, but only briefly. He had several lines hanging out of his mouth. He had two rusty hooks in his jaw. This old grouper had finally met his match, Mr. Bill! I can still see that smile on his face today. You know a smile that tells a hundred stories of how happy he was. He had waited all day for that fish and he had finally got it! The fish would hardly fit in the 100 quart cooler.

After all that, it was time to head for home. I was satisfied that the people would want to come again. However, Mr. Bill hadn't too much to say. I knew he was happy with that fish or, at least, I thought he was. It was a great trophy! On the way home he asked if I would be home tomorrow and I replied that I would. When we arrived home, everyone thanked me and said they had a good time and off they went with Mr. Bill.

Captain Bill Marsh showing off a fine red snapper.

The next morning, Bill Marsh did call and he booked around fifteen charters to start. He said there would be more. There were lots more! His business, The Hook and Line Tackle shop (located in Baxley, Georgia) might have been small, but it sure did have a lot of customers!

As the season flew by, Mr. Bill and I became best of friends. My father and him became real close. After all, they both had the same hair styles... My father was still running charters at the time. I think, at this time, his age was around eighty. Mr. Bill would go with him to help out on his trips. Mr. Bill was the only one who could get along with my father on his boat. He had experience in Florida with taking people fishing, so everything wasn't entirely new to him except for the way my father did things.

My father needed help on the boat and Mr. Bill was there to compliment him. At that time, Mr. Bill had sold his tackle business and had relocated in Savannah. He was staying with daddy and he was a great help. They found they had more in common than just the hair styles. They both loved to eat. They loved apple pie and ice cream. I mean the whole pie split in half and then there was the ice cream. They both loved television and, you guessed it, Gene Autry records. I like them myself. In fact, he is my Cowboy Hero!

Mr. Bill began helping my father a lot. Every week, every day, every minute, and then there was every second! Daddy like it. Mr. Bill was a great asset to him. He had found the son he never had. I think Mr. Bill was running the boat a long time before we knew it. My father trusted and loved him. He would find the fish and Mr. Bill would throw the buoy out to mark the spot which was hard to do with daddy still moving. Mr. Bill said sometimes he would stand by the fish finder and throw the buoy out long before my father shouted, "Let It Rip!" It didn't matter, they got the job done!

Mr. Bill decided to get his captain's license. It was time, he was definitely over qualified for the job. My father was going to retire, it was time, and now Captain Bill was ready to take over. He did a fine job! My father, however, still kept up with the status of his boat. No problem, Captain Bill always took good care of it, as if it were his own.

Captain Bill lived with my father and ran his boat for years. They made quite a team! After all, they kept the grocery store in business, all that hot apple pie and ice cream they shared together...

Captain Bill Marsh

FINDING THE BARNSTABLE

This day I will long remember…

We were fishing at the L buoy about 15 miles offshore of the Wassaw Sea buoy. The L buoy is a man made reef. It has sunken barges, tire, concrete pipe, and a few sunken pilot boats. It generally is very good fishing. You can usually get something to bite either on the top or bottom. Well, on this particular day, there wasn't anything biting. Believe me, we tried everything! I had mange to bore the customers beyond belief. I think they finally realized that there were no fish to be found in the ocean that day. I was totally convinced myself. We tried trolling and then we tried bottom fishing and even live lining. Nothing would even tease us. As I can remember, there wasn't any bait fish or any birds feeding. It was truly dead! I guess you get the picture by now.

I decided to go for pot luck. This is what you do when everything else fails. You put your lines out and troll the most ridiculous lures you can find. Use lures that have never worked or lures that you never tried because you knew nothing would ever touch them. We did just that. I started trolling toward the barn (home). I was making bout five to six knots. It was real calm, no breeze. We had left the L buoy about 45 minutes ago. I had the old fish finder on and it was just burning up that paper and the loran was clicking away. Slowly, we made our way toward home.

Scottie, my first mate, had about six lines out and he was trying everything he knew to make it look as though he was doing his best. It was certain the fish weren't going to help. The fish finder was showing a flat and not so interesting bottom. No fish at any depth. It looked like a desert down there. I had propped my feet up on the dash and you guessed it, I was doing some day dreaming.

All of a sudden, Scottie started screaming, "Fish on." I jumped up to see which line had been hit. As I did, all the lines started to peel off. It was amazing! We had six fish on at once. The boat was still moving and I reached to pull it out of gear and that is when I caught the fish finder out of the corner of my eye. My God, it was black. It was covered with fish from top to bottom. I quickly jotted down our TD's. Scottie was in the stern trying to gaff the fish as they came to the boat. I wasn't much help; I was busy trying to get all the TD's written down. All I could think was we are only in thirty-seven feet of water. What in the world have I run across?

I jumped down to help Scottie. We got four out of the six fish we hooked in the boat, which, by the way, are pretty good odds when fish being hooked are being hit by the fish that aren't. Every fish we brought to the boat had two or three following it, snapping at their tails. I looked over the side and all I could see was more fish. It looked like an aquarium. There were all types of fish. I spotted cobia, amberjack, king mackerel, Spanish mackerel, spade fish, barracuda, and that's just to name a few. We got the lines ready and put them back out. Oh, I forgot to tell you, we had boated two blue fish and two king mackerel. All the fish were of a nice size and not real common to this spot.

I made my circle and came around to the spot. This time, as I went over the area, I looked into the water and I saw hundreds of fish all swimming together. As soon as we went over the spot four more fish on. There were so many fish I couldn't tell if I had found a structure or just an unusual school of fish. I made a few passes to the right and left of the area. There were fish stacked everywhere you looked. I wrote down all TD's and marked every spot. I trolled over the area several times to make sure this wasn't just a school of fish. It was truly amazing!

My time was running out and we would have to leave soon. It's always good to catch the fish at the end of the day instead of the first of the day. The party seemed to forget how long it had taken to catch the big one.

As we were heading home, my mind was working into overtime. I was trying to guess what I had found. Was it an old sailing vessel or was it that old shrimp boat that went down and was never discovered? I couldn't wait for my next trip which was going to be tomorrow…

Well, tomorrow finally came and off we went. I knew I needed to keep this under my hat for a while or I would have too much company. At seven o'clock, everyone is pretty much leaving to start their fishing day, so I decided that I had better hold back and let all the other boats pass me by. I did.

To get to the new spot only took one hour and fifteen minutes from my dock. I had a full day trip and it was a gamble not going way off shore. What if they didn't bite? What if it was just an unusual school? I had to find out...

We pulled up to the spot and sure enough the same thing happened! We had fish on fish after fish. I decided to try some bottom fishing. I anchored the boat. I told Scottie that we were going to cut the anchor line if anyone headed to us. He agreed that we needed to keep this spot a secret for awhile. After getting the boat anchored, we got the bottom rigs out and baited them up. As fast as we let them out, we were bringing them back in. If you had three hooks, you got three fish and so on. We were catching fish so fast that there was a time that I only baited one hook. It didn't matter, I still got two fish. It didn't matter whether you had bait or not, so we decided to try all hooks without bait. You guessed it... for every hook, you got a fish. Believe me, it was unreal! And yes. It really happened the way I am telling you. I know it sounds far from the truth but it isn't. I kept looking into the water, it seemed as though I could see something but I couldn't make it out. It looked like rigging on a sailing vessel but then it looked like a mast head of some sort. I couldn't really tell at this point. Then I thought maybe I wanted to see something so bad I was starting to see things that weren't there.

Well, we had a great day! All the fish you could ever want. Sea bass, grouper, red snapper, silver snapper. All were Gulf Stream size. There were always turtles and dolphin around. It seemed as though it was their favorite fishing grounds. I was sure it was going to be mine.

I had many a great day at this spot. You look real good when you tell your party exactly what you are going to catch as soon as you put your line in the water. We caught a little bit of everything, top fish and bottom fish. I caught 7,000 pounds of fish off this spot over a period of five years.

I got the old chart out and started looking to see if any wrecks were listed in this area. Sure enough, there was but it wasn't quite where this one was located. I went to the spot marked on the chart and there wasn't any sign of a wreck there. I figured that there had been a mistake somewhere, but I wasn't real sure.

The first person I approached was Bill Walsh. I asked him if he knew of such a wreck and he said he hadn't ever done any diving in that area before. I asked him if he would take a look for me so I could determine what I had found and he did.

After his dive, he described to me the wreck and how it was located on the ocean floor. The ship was pointing northeast. It looked as though it might have been a ship built in the eighteen hundreds. She was all wooden and she was laid open with her ribs exposed. There was a big boiler and engine that looked as though it had fallen to the port side of the ship. The prop and shaft were laying there as if all you had to do was to build another boat around it and it would be ready to run again. There were two large anchors with tons of chain.

Bill said he had a hard time trying to see everything because of all the fish giving him the look over. He said, "There must be thousands of fish down there!"

Not knowing what I had found, I still continued to fish there almost every day, as long as there were no boats around. I never fished there on weekends because it was a straight shot to the sea buoy where everyone wanted to go and mostly did. Almost every time we fished this spot, we had great luck. This spot made fishing look so easy. Just put your line in the water and yes, you would get a fish on. I could tell you what you were going to catch, when you were going to catch it, and how to catch it. It was too good to be true!

One afternoon, I was talking to Captain Jim Bond and I told him about my findings and he said he would love to dive the area. Well, he did. He and his friends got the data plate off the vessel which enabled them to find out her real name and what her fate had been.

The name of the vessel was THE BARNSTABLE. She was 212 feetlong. She was a wooden steam vessel built in Trenton, Michigan in 1887. She was employed in commerce in the Great Lakes for a number of years. She later was assigned for coast wise service shortly before the war. The steam vessel was owned by Moore & McCormack of New York, but had been charted by the Taggart Coal Company and the Strachan Shipping Company. As we gathered all the information about the ship we were

The Barnstable before she came to rest in her shallow grave.

astonished at the letters that were sent through the mail before she made her fatal voyage to Havana with 1,000 tons of coal as her cargo. After leaving the port September 13, 1919 at Savannah, it seems as though she encountered heavy seas and high winds. As the storm began to get worse, the ship began to come apart. The articles that were printed in the newspaper told of the horrors that the crew faced as their vessel started floundering off of Savannah.

The northeast winds beat and pounded the ship until it started coming apart at the seams. The crew tried to keep her pumped out but the water was rushing in from the top and bottom. The waves had reached twenty feet. The crew had tried everything to keep her from going down but with everything going against them, they didn't have a chance. They had to abandon ship and get to the life boats. The first boat that was launched was damaged and lost by the heavy seas. The second one was successfully lowered and some of the crew was able to board. The wind quickly swept them away into the darkness. The third and last lifeboat was then lowered and the rest of the crew made their way to boarding it. They were also swept off into the darkness not knowing if the others had made it safely away from the floundering boat.

The newspaper article, that I found, told of the great horrors the crew faced after having to abandon ship. The first life boat to reach landfall had fifteen crew aboard. All were in pretty good shape. They had been tossed about for about eighteen hours. The second boat didn't have the best luck. They were washed ashore at Sapelo Island about forty-eight hours later. They had four men to bury when they arrived. All men who survived pretty much had the same story. The seas were over twenty feet and the boat just couldn't stay together. The seams started splitting and there wasn't any way to stay ahead of the incoming water. All efforts to save the vessel were put forth. Everyone worked together and there was no known panic. Everyone just simply did their job.

I found out the most interesting things when we started researching this vessel, once known as the Gettysburg, and the changed name being the BARNSTABLE.

This 212 foot wooden steamship, in my opinion, was doomed

long before its final sinking took place. This ship never seem to find it's honest place in the shipping world. The Gettysburg was first commissioned to work in intracoastal and great lakes trade. Later it was changed to ocean trade. The owners of this vessel had tried to sell her many times but the shipping commission would have no part in selling her to another country. She had always flown the American flag and this wasn't going to change, no matter what. At least, this was how I read it. And it didn't. She was going to fly our flag and she was going to do this above or below the surface!

The Gettysburg was built in 1887. Her name change was made in 1916 to the BARNSTABLE. The owner of the vessel wanted to sell her. By the end of the eighteen hundreds, she was in much need of major repair. They even had a buyer but the commissioner refused to let her be sold. At this time, she was only used for intracoastal and great lake commerce. The owners had to either spend more or lose a lot. So they did. They spent $90,000.00 and had her repaired and put into ocean trade. They were offered $300,000.00 for the BARNSTABLE before her repairs, but couldn't sell her. These numbers don't sound real to me, when you think that a boat 100' long now could cost up to $100,000.00 just for a few minor repairs.

The BARNSTABLE was ready to go. She was ready for the ocean. Now, for the next problem, no one would insure it. she wasn't really built for ocean going trade and I guess the insurance company knew that. The owners, once again, pleaded with the commission to let them sell the BARNSTABLE. The problem was that the only people interested were foreigners. As I said before, the BARNSTABLE could only be released to an American owned commerce. There was letter after letter written begging for the commission to release the BARNSTABLE to the foreign industry, but all this fell on deaf ears. I guess you could say, there was a lot of wasted paper flying around back in those days too!

The shipping board wasn't interested so they suggested that the navy might be and they transferred said letter to the navy for request. The poor BARNSTABLE, just sitting in port, waiting on her fate. The navy decided to use her for awhile but when the charted time ran out, they refused to renew their contract. The main complaint was that every time the vessel reached port, the crew being very unhappy with the vessel, would always transfer to another ship. This cost the navy money and loss of time.

The owners of the BARNSTABLE had to do something, so they did. They got a charter to haul coal to Cuba from Savannah. The ship was loaded with 1,300 tons of coal and headed out September 13, 1919 in a brisk breeze which gradually increased in violence, as the vessel proceeded. The vessel later sunk that night twenty miles southeast of Tybee Light.

I have put together some interesting facts that happened after the sinking of the S.S. BARNSTABLE.

There were suppose to be a total of twenty-seven crew men aboard the ship, all were accounted for including the four that were deceased at the time of arrival to Sapelo Island. However, two days after the sinking, the ITASCA (another ship) removed a man out of the rigging of the BARNSTABLE. If all crew was accounted for, where did this body come from? The ship was apparently drifting or was it just bottomed out and that much was above the surface?

The YARACRAW (a ship) sighted the wreck, the mast still standing, came back later to blow it up but failed to find it.

A partially sunken wooden vessel is reported to have been destroyed by a torpedo, not sure, but it was reported. I wonder which boat they sunk. It doesn't seem to be the BARNSTABLE.

Two years later, after tons of paper work and maintenance of a gas lighted buoy that was only put in the area, and several attempts to find and destroy the BARNSTABLE, nothing had changed. The gas lighted buoy that only make the area of the BARNSTABLE was still being maintained and ships were giving the buoy at least a berth of a mile clearance. The ship had yet been found or destroyed.

On May 10, 1921, the SEMINOLE sailed from Wilmington, North Carolina on a voyage to the area where the BARNSTABLE was supposed to be located. Her mission was to search and find, then destroy the BARNSTABLE that was such a menace to navigation. My question is, "How can something be a navigational hazard if no one can find it?" I am sure that there were thoughts that maybe this was a small area of the Devil's Triangle. After all, no one had hit it for two years. I think the odds were getting less and less that this was going to happen. The SEMINOLE was able to receive help from aircraft in hopes to site the BARNSTABLE. However, the ship was radioed later that the weather was unfit for flying. There would be no aircraft to aid the ship in its search.

The SEMINOLE lowered two boats and they searched with grapnels and water glass. For three days these operations continued. No luck and no BARNSTABLE.

The navy put two naval hydroplanes up at different altitudes. This turned out to be unsuccessful. One of the naval planes had engine trouble and had to be towed into port for repairs. I think the BARNSTABLE had a mind of its own. It had just disappeared.

Finally on July 1, 1921, the search for the BARNSTABLE was discontinued. There she lays in forty-two feet of water and until 1986, her masthead was still standing. Her anchor was still out and holding. Her spare anchor is still there and waiting to be called for duty. She is a little spread out, but who cares. She deserves a rest and it's so peaceful where she lies. Her crew never wants to leave her side. They have changed from men to fish. They seem to love her and she has finally found her place... I feel like I know her!

The Miss Judy Too assissting in the sinking of the Motherlode.

RUMORS BEGAN TO FLY

To find a wreck is really an interesting thing to do. Your imagination runs wild. In the late seventies, a two engine plane crashed offshore about sixteen miles. My father was fishing in that area when the crash occurred. I was inshore of his location doing some trolling. As soon as we heard of the accident, all boats hurried to the area to see if there were any survivors. Well, unfortunately, there were none. One charter boat, out of Hilton Head, South Carolina, found the floating fuselage. Luckily, he got the numbers and reported it to the coast guard. He said there was no chance of any survivors. My father arrived and before everyone's eyes, the airplane vanished into its temporary grave. Boats picked up an airplane tire, a woman's purse, and other unidentified parts of the crashed plane.

At this point, no one knew how many passengers were involved or where they were headed. Everyone just said, "The plane just seem to fall out of the sky." That night my phone began ringing. People were calling, trying to get information on the location of the wreck. I didn't know any of the parties calling so, of course, I wasn't about to give out any information. RUMORS BEGAN TO FLY!

One story I heard was the plane was carrying laundered money from Atlantic City to somewhere south. Well, I did get a lot of inquiries about the location and lots of people were looking for the remains of this plane for some reason.
Another story was the plane was supposed to be carrying a fugitive. The plane was blown up so that the fugitive would supposedly be dead. Who knows? I guess it could be possible.

Bill Walsh, a good friend of mine, worked with the coast guard getting all the information on the plane as it lay on the ocean floor. Bill slipped into the water and descended down. As he approached the ocean floor, he said that he passed through several layers of murky colored water. When he was twenty feet from the bottom, he got the real picture of the plane or, should I say, what was left of the plane. As he explored, he found other parts. He found human bones laying about the area. These had been picked clean and had become part of the food chain. As he began removing the pieces, he found hands and feet wedged under the debris.

Can you imagine being down sixty feet, looking around, and finding that? Later that day, the coast guard picked up half of a headless torso with his neck tie still attached to what was left of his neck.

Bill retrieved most of the wreckage so, hopefully, someone could determine what might have happened. I never did find out. There is still some of that old unanswered airplane down there just making up its own natural reef...

It's a great place to catch king and Spanish mackerel. I have even caught a few bottom fish there. I think I mentioned it was only in sixty feet of water, didn't I?

GEORGIA STATE RECORDS

TRIGGER FISH

Bonnie and Clyde (Beth and Ralph Zeagler) frequent our service three or four times a year. I first met them on their honeymoon trip to Savannah. We have become great friends and fishing buddies since.

I named them Bonnie and Clyde because they always drive up in a black Cadillac with tinted windows and a machine gun under the seat. I have even shot it once or twice!

This duo has caught about every kind of fish this area offers. In fact, Beth holds the Georgia Women's State Record for the largest trigger fish. This baby weighed in at 11 pounds 5 ounces. She caught it while we were fishing the Savannah snapper banks. When Bonnie and Clyde come down to do some fishing, it is serious business. They are always up for what's biting and will even go for the ones you have to wait for. We were fishing for grouper the day she caught her record. Beth is now ready to go for number two and is looking for it in 1992...

Bonnie and Clyde Zeagler.

Beth Zeagler showing off her Georgia State Record trigger fish.

Roger Erb holding his world record trigger fish.

Roger Erb, his family, and friends fish with me regularly. They are great fishermen. They love just being out in the water and fishing is a special extra. Roger holds the Georgia Men's State Record for trigger fish. His trigger was not only a state record, but it was also a world record. Roger's fish weighed 10 pounds 9 ounces and was also caught at the Savannah snapper banks.

RED DRUM

The Prices, from Atlanta, charted my boat and had a very interesting day…. The charter was a gift from each of them. They had a blast! Both were fishing steadily. We got into the spottail bass and they both caught several. The exciting part was they both broke the Men's and Women's Georgia State Records for red drum (spottail bass). The same day – same time – from the same school. Mrs. Price red drum weighed 38 pounds 13.5 ounces. Mr. Price's red drum weighed 46 pounds 7 ounces. Both fish were landed in November of 1986. These fish are tough fighters and they had a good time landing them. Spottail bass are also called red drum, channel bass, or stag bass.

Sandra and Richard Price display their trophy fish with Captain Judy Helmey and first mate Ali.

WAHOO

Tommy Earl Pope caught a real large wahoo that easily broke the Men's Georgia Record. His fish weighed 91 pounds 8 ounces. We caught this fish while live lining at the north snapper banks. Tommy fought this wahoo forty-five minutes before landing it. I chased this fish for fifteen minutes just so we could catch up with his forward motion. Boy, this was a trophy! This was a BIG fish! Tommy, thank goodness, was more determined to get him in than the fish was to get away. Tommy never let off. He kept the line tight and never once gave this fish any slack.

As we watched, this fish swam around frantically trying to throw the hook. We had a little uninvited company.... Yes, Mr. Shark or I might say Mr. Huge Shark was now stalking our soon to be record or his soon to be lunch. This shark went crazy and the fish with what little fight he had left, also went crazy.

Big shark, big fish, and Tommy just reeling, trying to beat the inevitable future. We all knew if the shark even touched or attached the wahoo our chances of a record would be lost.

Tommy really put the steam on and maneuvered the fish so that we could get a safe chance with the gaff. Matt Starling, my first mate, did a fine job. This fish had two problems, us and the shark. When he dove, the shark was there and when he surfaced, we were there. He finally came too close and Matt made a long reach and pulled this 115 pounder aboard. Just as Matt gaffed the fish, he pitched his head and the rig came flying out. The hook buried itself in the closest thing, a fisherman's leg. Thank goodness, the hook didn't go past the barb. The fisherman, before thinking, just reach down and pulled the hook out bringing quite a large portion of flesh.

The fish was finally in the boat. It had been almost two hours since we hooked this monster. After everybody had calmed down and we had done what first aid we could to the hole in his leg, we weighed the fish. We were all very shocked! This wahoo weighed over 115 pounds. I know I said he only weighed 91 pounds, that was after he had been sitting all day.

I knew this fish would lose some weight, but we tried to keep him as cold as possible. I didn't have a big enough cooler to put

Tommy Earl Pope standing by his state record wahoo weighing 91 pounds.

him in so we wrapped him up in some towels and put bags of ice around him. When we arrived to get him weighed, he was 91 pounds. He was still a very enormous fish. This wahoo had a big open ulcer on his tail and it was draining the whole time. That didn't help, it only hurt the weight.

SAND BAR TIGER SHARK

Clara Adams holds the Women's Georgia State Record for the large Sand Bar Tiger Shark. This shark weighed in at 212 pounds 6 ounces.

We were fishing at the K C Buoy, located about five miles east of the Wassaw sea buoy. We were doing a little bottom fishing at the time and the fish weren't biting so well. I think we figured out why! Clara had brought her a new 6/0 Penn reel and rod to match. She was ready for the big one. We wanted to break it in right, however, we had no idea that a 212 pound shark was going to pay us a visit that day...

Clara had put her bottom rig out and was half way paying attention to it and the other half of her attention was on her boyfriend, who was making a bet with her about who was going to catch the biggest fish. Yes, the betting was going on and so was the fishing. Neither of the two was getting very far.

Clara's line looked as though it had gotten hung up on the bottom. The line tightened up a little bit, but then it started moving, Clara picked up her rod and set the hook. This shark seemed to be real calm until he found out he was hooked and off she went with about 200 yards of line. Yes, I said 200 yards of line! Clara's eyes were getting larger as the line peeled off.

Clara and her new rod and reel were in for a real work out. This escapade lasted about two and a half hours. This was before we even got a chance to gaff this big shark.

The gaffing of a shark was quite a treat! Ida Knight, my first mate, was helping me that day. After seeing this shark swim by the boat, we both said we needed to get a larger boat. Clara got the shark to the surface several times and he would just take off on another long run. All Ida and I could think was please get this fish real tired before we have to deal with it. Ida and I had decided what we were going to do. First, we were going to gaff him, then I was going to try to shoot him. Ida was going to lasso the shark's tail and I was going to pull him backwards and drown him. Well, that all sounded so good, however, plans are made to change and usually do. We tried to gaff this sea monster more than one. Yes, we made contact only briefly and the shark would just roll off the gaff. Another step we were going to try was shooting this big boy. Well, that avenue closed as soon as we found out this shark probably was a record. So using the gun was out of the question. It was just me and Captain Ida. Believe me, I wanted it to be more Captain Ida than me!

As I said, the gaff would not stay. The shark would just roll and the gaff would come free. As the shark rolled he would almost drown everyone on the boat. Ida came up with the idea of sticking the gaff down his throat. I laughed, "What do you want me to do? Tell the shark to say AAH!" Well, we finally made contact and got the lasso around the shark's tail. We drowned the shark by pulling it behind the boat. I pulled it an extra long time just to make sure.

After getting the shark to the boat, everyone was very tired. Clara's rod and reel really had a work out and so did Clara. It was now time for her to collect her bet. I never really knew what the bet was, but I was sure of one thing. Clara's fish was definitely the best catch of the day!

Captain Judy and Clara Adams showing off their 212 pound Sand Bar Tiger Shark

Happy fishermen show off their catch. (left to right) Ricky Corley, David Sanders, Larry Clegg, Mark Yarbrough, Steve Dyer, and Chris Tackett.

In Appreciation to
Miss Judy Charter's Fishing Team

Captain Judy, angler, and Matt Starling showing off big red snapper.

Ivory Durden with tons of red snapper.

Paul Roundtree holding his two forty pound amberjack.

Lamar Tuten, Captian Judy, and Dr. Dixie Wade displaying their fine red snappers caught on the Miss Judy Too.

Captain Ali and David (Bones) Bolden of the Magnificent Seven Fishing Club displaying his king mackerel

Matt Starling showing off his large king mackerel.

Charlie Baker displaying his red snapper.

Captain Ida displaying a large red snapper.

Left to Right: Smokey Kloss, Jim Johnson, Captain Judy, Scott, Dale Mettler. What a day!

Captain Ida Knight unloading their fine catch.

James Doyle with his fine catch of barracuda and king mackerel.

Tony Bettis showing off his 198 pound nurse shark.

Vic Starling gaffing a king mackerel.

Father and son, Pilkington, showing off catch.

Captain Ida holding new born tiger shark.

Another great day on the Miss Judy Too!

Al Nevarez and Captain Judy showing off large barracuda.

Fish Up!

Al Askew and party proud of their catch.

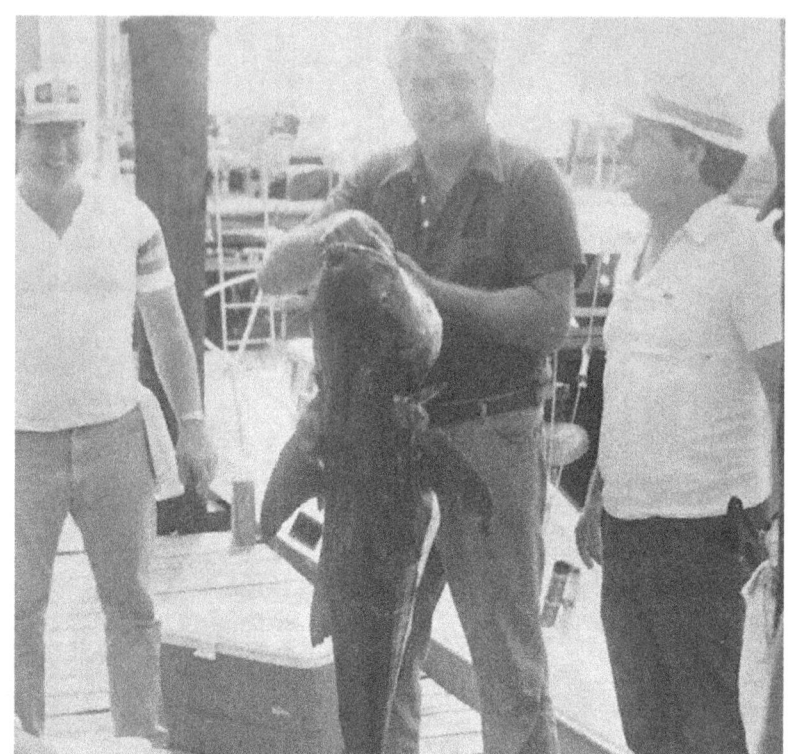

These fishermen are proud of their fine catch.

Chris Gapner holding his barracuda caught on the Miss Judy Too.

Mrs. Parson is proud of her prize barracuda.

Fishing is fun on the Miss Judy Too.

A happy fisherman displaying his bull dolphin.

Hooked up again!

First mate, Captain Ali and fishing party holding amberjack.

Come go fishing on the Miss Judy Too.

INTRIGUING FISH

I've chose several strange fish to catch you up on:

Flounder, halibut or ocean pancakes (as I call them) are most common in this area. They go through drastic changes from birth to adulthood. They are born looking like normal fish, not flat. Gradually, as they age, the fish begin to lean to one side. The mouth and lower eye move to join the other eye on the top side. After this process, they mainly stay on the bottom unless they are travelling or feeding. They are capable of changing to any background color they are laying on. They can turn red, blue, etc… whatever the ocean floor color may be. Ocean pancakes are delicious cooked many ways. My favorite is fried, topped with syrup.

Talk about having a big head… the ocean sunfish or head fish consist mainly of a head. Picture a 400 pound fish with an upper and lower fin that looks like someone took a pair of pinking shears and cut his body off. The fins are quite large. From a distance, the upper fin might look like the dorsal fin of a shark. The closer you get, you notice how limber it is. They flap around with the movement of the sea. It almost looks as though they are waving at you as you pass by. Ocean fish seem to have very little mobility. I mean after all, if they don't have a tail, how could they possibly get the momentum to leap into the air. Well, let me tell you, they can do just that. I have seen them leap completely out of the water and turn in mid air. A most unbelievable site to behold! These beautiful creatures of the sea do not have any food value. I don't think I have enough syrup anyway.

The toad fish, more commonly known as the dog fish, are just plain ugly. They have a set of jaws that are capable of cracking oysters for lunch. The females usually spawn in the summer time. The males are responsible for guarding the eggs. They usually put them in an old can or a discarded shell. While they are on duty they are very vicious.

We catch small to very large toads offshore. The inshore fish are dark green with spots. The offshore toads are a rusty color with spots and are much larger. We usually catch them when the drift is slow or if the boat is anchored. They are considered bottom dwellers.

Toad fish are very ugly, but believe it or not, I have eaten them before. You remove the skin as you would skin a catfish. You remove the entrails and then you have a drumstick shape piece of very white meat. Batter it and deep fry it. It's very good. I know what you're saying. I would never touch one much less clean and cook it! Well, if you have ever been to one of our fish fries then you probably have already had this fish. I love serving them to my guests...

Remoras, also referred to as pilot sharks, shark suckers, or scavenger fish. These fish have a suction disc located on top of their hear. They use this disc to attach themselves below the mouth so they can get their free meal. Remoras are not considered to be parasites, they just attach for the leftovers and the free ride. They are very common free loaders to sharks, marlin, swordfish, amberjack, turtles, and many more.

They will hang around the boat sometimes as though they know they might get a free meal. Mostly they travel in pairs. If you hold a piece of squid over the side, they will stick their head up out of the water and take it right out of your hand. They do not look like dolphin but in some instances, they tend to act like them. When they pop their head out of the water it's as if they are going to say something.

The goose fish may give us anglers a run for our catch. They have built in rods located on the top of their head. This rod is equipped with its own bait. The fish dangles the bait to attract its prey. Goose fish don't go hunting for their food, they just lay very still, dangle their bait, and at the right time, they open up their mouth and suck in their prey. What I just described to you sounds like a pretty macho fish doesn't it? They don't get over ten pounds. I bet their catch ratio is higher than ours.

Here is another fish that has quite a background. It is not very large or it appears to be real small, about the size of a small croaker. However, this fish is capable of blowing its belly up with air whenever it feels that danger is near. This of course would probably scare off the biggest of fishes. This fish is called a Puffer fish. We catch them a lot at the snapper banks. They always amuse the customers. As soon as you touch them, they inflate themselves up. If you listen before they start to inflate, they make a sound like an air pump sucking in air. When you release them back to the water, they blow around on the surface like a balloon. After a few seconds of that, they just deflate and off to the bottom they go.

I have tasted the puffer before and they are good. There isn't much meat on a fish of that size. I prefer to let them go and scare their enemy to death...

We catch quite a few Parrot fish. They are quite small, less than 10" long. Don't let the size throw you, they have a set of teeth that are equal to a hole punch. Be sure to keep your fingers clear of their mouth. They are beautiful! They wear the colors of a parrot. When you watch them, they will change colors before your eyes. They will change maybe from light blue to a bright red and yellow. If possible, I always try to let them go unharmed.

The Lady fish which I sometimes refer to as the miniature Tarpon. They seem to enjoy jumping out of the water as much as they do swimming in it. I have seen a Lady fish jump out of the water even with a sixteen ounce sinker tied to the rig. They are lots of fun to catch. Always let them go as soon as you remove the hook. They don't last too long out of the water. This is one fish we need to keep around.

One of the most asked questions on the boat is, "Is there such a thing as a Flying fish?" When I answer yes, they seem to be relieved that what they just saw was not just a wave or their imagination running wild. We have an abundance of them in our area. They seem to take flight when something large is after them. They glide along using part of their tail as a rudder. Sometimes you will see just one or two or you may see a whole school flying together. Their slender shape resembled that of skinny mullet with wings. They have been known to fly right into the boat. This is good and free bait. If this happens, we use them for king mackerel and bull dolphin.

We catch a brownish fish that has its own built in hard hat. It is called a Sea Robin. This fish also comes equipped with wigs, but it doesn't use these to take flight. They are used for hovering over the bottom looking for their next meal. They make a real good conversation piece. Their head is as hard as that of a helmet and their wings are quite large. Their helmet comes equipped with its own built in swords that point to the stern of the fish. Surely any fish that would try to eat this fish would have to be very hungry.

When I started fishing, black fish (sea bass) were almost in abundance everywhere. Well, twenty-five years later and thank God we still have some, although, they are not as heavily concentrated as they use to be. And with that last statement, I am sure there will be plenty of remarks like this: "This woman is crazy, there are black fish everywhere, hundreds of thousands!" I love those types of people because they can't help the way they feel...

Sea bass will eat almost anything you throw at them. They are bottom feeders. Anything that comes across their mouth is sure to be their supper. We have caught sea bass with chicken bones, bubble gum, and plain old rubber worms. (Any color of worm will do.) however, they do feed in patterns. Sometimes they will bite all day and other times they seem to just be sleeping. I guess we all have to do that sometimes. Sea bass are related to the grouper family. They even look like a grouper with their large head and big mouth. As I said, they will put almost anything in their mouth and try to consume it.

The best time to catch bass is in the spring and fall months. They spawn in the spring. Sea bass mature as a female. In about three years, they turn into a male. How about that! Most of the smaller bass you catch are females. They don't have much color; however, the bigger males have large humps on their back with streaks of blue. The humps on the males are caused from stress. The stress of having to fertilize all those eggs. Those eggs being over 100,000 per female. Some job!

Sea bass are generally caught in 30 to 100 feet of water. You can also find large amounts around wrecks. They seem to hide in all those areas where they think no one can get to them. They will sometimes swim up to feed on schools of shrimp or any other bait.

I use squid and cut fish mostly for bait. Sometimes when they are really hungry you can get two or more fish on one hook. They are very good to eat. They are not boney and don't have a strong taste. I love them deep fried. Oh, by the way, I pour syrup on all my fish. It's so good!

ENTICING BOTTOM BAITS

Fishing on the bottom is a very popular type of fishing because you never really know what you might catch. The Savannah snapper banks has a great live bottom which consist of coral, plant vegetation, and high ledges. All these make up the ocean floor located thirty miles off Savannah's coast.

All types of bottom feeders are there just waiting for you to drop them a line. I use mostly squid for bait. They seem to like it the best. They also know how to take it off the hook fast. Cut bait is very effective and it stays on the hook better. We use cigar minnows and Spanish sardines. They are most effective when there are large snapper and grouper around. Another way to get that big one is to hook a small vermillion by his lips and send him down to the bottom. You can be sure if a snapper or grouper is in seeing distance he will knock on your door. When I fish with the customers, I always use this bait. It is real effective. I might not catch ten, but I always get a big one and that's what everyone wants. That's when they forget they caught a hundred small ones and just look at the big ones!

I also use BUTTERFLY BAIT. This is a small fish, such as a vermillion snapper, rock bass, or small blackfish. You cut their backbone out, the two sides of meat just flow with the currents and it also attracts large fish.

I cannot lie. I have left the dock without my bait before. By the time I realized I didn't have it, it would be too late to turn around. I have used some pretty off the wall baits! All you need is a small fish to cut up and you are in business. If this happens to you, here are some pointers. Everyone has lunch, so just put some of that ham on a hook and give it a try. Chicken isn't too bad either. Chewing gum is good bait; it stays on the hook real well. A piece of white cloth, cut into strips will work also. Believe it or not, this will work trolling too! So just think about it even if you run out of bait, there are still plenty of options.

We primarily use squid for bait. I use it for bottom fishing and even sometimes for trolling. I have eaten it raw before. I should try it if the fish like it. I have to understand why they like it, don't I? I sure wouldn't want to make a meal of it! One piece will do you. I have tried it fried and that's not too bad. All you have to do is batter it and deep fry it. Oh, you best clean it first. The best way to do it is to put it on the hook and forget about supper!

The squid we use for bait is the same squid you might get in a restaurant. The only difference is that they clean it before they cook it. We just cut it up in little pieces and put it on the hook and the fish just love it for their dinner. Fish love squid and will take it almost every time. Even when they are not biting too well, they are always up for that squid taste.

We often dissect a squid for our customers. I like to show them the backbone of the squid. It always fascinated everyone. It looks as if it is made of plastic. I have even been asked why we put the plastic in the squid. I did a little research on squid and I found some pretty interesting things about a creature that doesn't seem to amount to much.

Squid only mate once in their lifetime. After this ritual, both male and female die. The female carries the eggs in a cavity under the eye or in a cavity under its neck. Different species of squid carry their eggs different. The female deposits the fertilized eggs on a rock or they just float in the open sea. Young squid hatch as small miniature adults. They are ready to survive on their own. Some full grown squid are less than one inch while others grow to be sixty feet long!

Squid are considered a predator. I know your saying, "A small piece of bait, a predator?" Well, it's true. The squid has eight arms. It also has two extra arms that are especially great in aiding the squid to get his next picked meal. The two extra arms are able to reach out and grab their unsuspecting prey. These arms are equipped with suckers or little hooks. They reach out and snatch their prey and bring it close so that the other eight arms can take over. Their arms hold the prey near their mouth and their parrot like beak mouth tears it apart. No remember, I am talking about a squid that is only one inch long.

Squid are very fast. They don't flap their wings or their tails. They move, I guess you could say, by jet propulsion. The squid draws in water and then ejects it through its funnel. This moves the squid quickly in the direction he has chosen.

Squid have a very unique way of camouflaging themselves. When in danger, they can eject a black cloud in their image. As the black cloud disperses, the squid is long gone out of the area.

I have summed up everything that I have find out about the squid. They definitely have more arms than we do. Their arms are equipped with their own fishing tackle. As small as they are, they can crush their prey with their very powerful mouth. They swim in a backwards like motion. They can change color for camouflaging. They can even eject a smoke screen that will cover their tracks. Does that sound like something from our planet? All these capabilities in one inch!

Have you ever heard of asafetida (as a fet'i da)? What the heck is that, right? That's what I said. A friend of mine, Charlie Eden, told me about asafetida.

Asafetida is an old timey drug. It was formerly used in medicine as a sedative, especially in spasms and convulsions. It comes from the root of an asafetida plant. The milk juice which is removed from the root is used in making this gum like drug. The drug has a very offensive odor. People would hang this drug around their neck. With its god awful odor, it would supposedly ward off contagious diseases. My answer to that, "Who knows if the drug worked? No one would ever get that close to the odor!"

Charlie told me to take this drug and melt it in some water. Then take some small rags, dip them in it and use the rags for bait. He said the fish would go crazy. "Don't you like a good fish story? I know I do!" Well, this is no story.

Charlie took me to the lake and proved it. The fish did go crazy. They chased the strips of rags and tried to eat them. It was unbelievable!

Yes, you know what I'm thinking. I bought me some from the local pharmacy. I went through the process, dipped the rags and so on. I thought a real test would be to try it off my dock. I did. It worked! The catfish would follow the rags to the surface. It was unbelievable! I never tried it offshore for one good reason. I just couldn't get pass the smell…

119

A proud display of Chopper Blues.

CHOPPER BLUES

Blue fish migrate to this area in the spring of the year. There are two names for this fish. The smaller fish are called School Blues. They range from one to three pounds and are approximately one to three years old. The larger blues are called CHOPPERS. They range from 10 to 15 pounds and live up to ten years of age.

Although both sizes travel in schools, the School Blues travel in greater numbers than the CHOPPERS. School Blues are usually accompanied by the smell of cucumbers and melons. I am not sure if it is the bait fish the blues feed on or it the blues are secreting a slick that produces the smell. You can be sure this smell means the blue fish are there.

One good way to spot a school of clues is to look for bird action. The blues are driving the frantic bait up while the birds are attacking from above. Try to troll or cast to the edges of the school. Running through the school might breakup or spook their feeding. On a calm day, you can probably spot the bait fish and the splashing of the blues attacking. On a rough day, they tend to feed a little deeper.

The CHOPPERS live up to their name by the way they thrash at the bait with their very distinctive set of needle sharp teeth. I have found out the hard way that this name is appropriate from the scars I have. Dead or alive, their teeth are as sharp as a razor.

Sometimes referred to as "LEFTY," the CHOPPERS are left-eyed. The blue fish will normally approach its meal with its left eye focused on its prey. If possible, when presenting the bait, throw it to the left side of the fish or school.

If you are fishing for blues around a wreck, the best thing to do is anchor above the wreck so the bait will drift over it. You can also chum for them by throwing out small fish or squid. It doesn't take a lot to get their attention. Believe me, all they want to do is eat.

When they are feeding, you can count on them hitting anything you through at them. If your hitting slows down, switch to a larger bait. Ecls, cigar minnows, squid, and live fish seem to be their most popular bait. I have used sea witches, silver spoons (all sizes), and even the cisco kid. You can purchase most of these lures at your local tackle store.

When we catch the CHOPPERS, we always cut their throat. This let the fish bleed and it takes the blood line out of the fish. The blood line in most fish aren't as big as the blues. If you try this method, you will find that the meat is a lot whiter and cleaner. When cleaning the fish, we just filet them on each side and then cut the skin off. The blood line is located just below the skin from the head to the tail of each side. If you forget to bleed the fish, just cut the blood line out. It's not too much extra work. The blood line is dark and it tastes stronger than the meat. Blues are good fried, baked, but best to me is when they are smoked. If excitement is what you are looking for early in the season, the BLUES will certainly be worth your while.

FISH DO THE DARNDEST THINGS

One spring morning, as usual, we started on our next venture to tame the wild ocean. Jackie Sommers had chartered the boat and we were going out to do some live lining for king mackerel and blue fish. Jackie has been fishing with me for years and it would seem if something strange would happen, it would happen to him.

We were going to the L Buoy and do some trolling for Spanish mackerel. We were doing quite well. Every time we passed over the Henry Bacon, a sunken pilot ship, we would hook up a Spanish. I kept noticing a large shinny fish hanging around the Bacon every time we made a pass. It looked to be about a five foot cuda. This is a fish that Jackie loves to catch. He likes to feed the Spanish to them. It's a lot of fun trying to get the cuda hooked up.

Barracuda usually strike on eye site. The cuda's first hit usually cuts the bait in half and then they come back and pick up the pieces until they are all gone.

Jackie had his bait rigged up and ready to go. He presented the bait to the fish. I could see from the bridge that the cuda was definitely interested. The fish perked up immediate as he pulled the bait by him. The fish's first dart at the bait was a miss. The fish has misjudged the speed I was trolling. He then turned and headed straight for the bait. This time he cut it in half. Jackie immediately released the line to let the remaining bait sink, the cuda returned and took the leftovers. The fight was on, the cuda leaped in and out of the water. After his fifth jump, he finally managed to fray the line and he got the bait, hooks, and ten feet of line.

We immediately rigged another bait up. Usually after a fish has just been hooked, they are not interested in eating any more for awhile. When they get hooked, they get excited trying to swim away from the pressure. There is a form of acid that build up when the fish is in a "Feeding Frenzy." This acid covers the muscles and it slows them down, rest is the only way to correct this problem.

However, this was not the case for this particular fish. We presented the bait as before; the fish came from nowhere and took the bait. This time we thought we might get him. We fought him for about six to seven minutes. The cuda was still more in the air than in the water. Jackie always managed to keep the line tight. The fish jumped the last time and then sounded. He headed straight for the boat, the line became slack, it happened so fast. Jackie quickly took the slack out. This smart fish had just made a great show and now it was time for him to go somewhere else and he did, leaving us with only empty hooks, or at least that what we thought we had. Jackie brought the line in and we did have hooks and more hooks. More than we started out with! Yes, we had the original rig that the fish had gotten and then we had our present hooks. And yes, this fish had showed us that maybe they knew more than we give them credit for! At least he returned them after he made his point…

A seafood smorgasboard caught on the Miss Judy Too.

PLAYING THE FISH

Playing the fish demands a give and take battle. This is why it is important to use the right type of line and tie the right knot. I prefer to use pre-stretched mono filament line and the cinch knot. In the following paragraphs, I will explain my techniques for landing a fish.

The best way to set a hook is to use a series of short, sharp jerks in rapid succession. Try to keep the line tight. A hooked fish is instinctive defense is to seek the safety of anything it can swim into, under, or around. Always remember to check the tension set on your reel, it should never be completely locked down. The tension should be set so that if the fish takes a run, the line won't break. The key is to cushion the shock on the line without yielding to the fish. Some fish will stop pulling if there is a sudden release of tension on the line. Too much slack gives your hooked fish a chance to throw the hook or swim off the hook.

In fighting a fish, beginners often let excitement cloud their judgment. Their first reaction is to jerk up on the rod and try to reel at the same time. This is called pumping the fish the wrong way. Pumping is performed by gingerly, but precisely pulling up the rod and reeling in the slack as you drop the rod down.

Certain species of fish are spectacular jumpers and can add pressure up to the line. When confronted with a jumping fish, exercise caution. Point your rod toward the fish, creating controlled slack in the line. As the fish falls back into the water, you can then gain control. This is called BOWING to the fish.

The most critical point of the struggle occurs when the fish is close to the boat. You have less line out to cushion the strain. After seeing the boat, a fish will usually take one or more runs. I have a very special name for fish that are very active. This fish is still "VERY GREEN."

You are now ready to land your fish. The most common methods are netting or gaffing. When netting, simply hold the net in front of the fish and lead him into the net. I have never seen a fish that can swim backwards yet. Gaffing is a bit more difficult. You must position the gaff under the fish without letting the handle get in front of the line or leader. When in this position, pull up and toward yourself quickly! Then lift your fish into the boat. I always have my cooler open and ready to throw the fish in.

It is always good to check your line, leader, and hooks after each bite. Lines have a tendency to get cut or nicks. Leaders and hooks once bent become considerably weaker.

These few steps I have listed are good to follow, but you need to remember to be careful with fish that are incoming on the gaff. Hooks can become free with the fish thrashing, which can result in injury to you or others. I have had this happen to me a few times and believe me it doesn't feel very good.

FEATHERED FRIENDS AND THEIR EXTRAORDINARY PAST

Offshore, you see many interesting and unusual birds. One of these birds is known as the cormorant. We see these birds mostly in the spring and fall. You can get very close to them; they won't even try to fly away. They jump, flap their wings, and splash away from us. They are deep divers, going down in search of their favorite seafood delight. These birds have long bills, which enables them to catch more than a mouthful at a time.

Many years ago, it was said that these birds played a very big part in commercial fishing in Japan. The fisherman would catch a few of these birds and put rings around their necks to stop the bird from swallowing what he caught. They would attach a line to the foot, which would not allow them to swim off. The commercial fishermen would hang their large wire baskets out, fill them up with wood, and light it up. The fire would attract the fish and the birds would catch them. I think I would rather catch them myself. At any rate, this is how it use to be. I guess this was before fishing became a real sport...

Throughout the years I have been fishing, I have noticed different types of birds migrating in and out of our area. There are many different types other than the seabirds we see every day at the beach. These birds never come to land unless they are mating or having their young.

I got an opportunity to view a few of these wonderful birds. The most unusual was the "WOMPUS BOOBY." Better known as the "BROWN BOOBY." There's a very interesting story behind its name. The name wompus, derived from sailors at sea. These birds would land on the ship, and they would just lay there while the sailor beat them to death. No, don't think sailors are just playing mean, They're not. This took place in the 1800's on old sailing vessels, these birds were a source of diet for the crew.

When I was in Central America fishing, a brown booby landed on our boat. A beautiful bird it was! This bird was not afraid of humans. You could move about the bird and even touch him. The bird didn't seem to be bothered a bit. He was real happy just to have a place to rest.

Wompus Boobie.

There is another bird that migrates in our area in the fall and winter months. I called these birds "FOLLOW UPS." They travel in flocks of fifteen or less. They are very small birds and they look like miniature mallards. I also call them "Baby Ducks." They land on the water and look just like little ducks, fully mature ducks, it's amazing!

Most birds that stay offshore can be easily recognized. They don't seem to fly real high. They stay close to the water below the horizon. They are riding the winds right above the water. They seem to glide along not using much energy to do so.

My father told me a few old myths about seabirds...

Seagulls are said to be possessed by the spirits of "DEAD SEA-MEN."

Some seabirds were believed to hatch from the shells of barnacles.

Some of the statements sounded like they were made up after a bottle of "GROG" was passed around a few too many times. In my father's case, a bottle of "OLD CROW."

A nice sail fish caught by Captain Judy and Captain Ali.

PREDICTING WEATHER NATURES WAY

I was not educated to be able to professionally predict the weather. Being around the ocean as much as I am, you tend to pick up little hints of what your next weather pattern might be. You wouldn't believe all the signs out there that help you make your own forecast.

When my father was fishing, he would always say, "See those flies." I would always notice them but would never realize there importance. He would say, "There will be a northeasterly wind blowing within three days." Most of the time, he was right.

It is true. I have been offshore forty miles from any land and have been attacked by hundreds of flies. They look like regular houseflies, but they are not. They BITE. I mean, even through your clothing. Bug spray doesn't even seem to affect them. At any rate, you can be sure your daily income is going to decline, "No fishing, no money!" There would be plenty of wind that would last either three, six, or nine days.

My father had another saying, "Well the fish have the sore mouth today." After that, you would hear about a cold front approaching. The fish would take the bait, but they would not bite down on it. It was almost as if they did bite down but it hurt their mouth. I guess fish have sinus problems just like us.

When you have high wind approaching from far away, such as a hurricane, the ocean seems to swell up. It looks very different than it does twenty-five knot northeast wind blows. The ocean seems dark even when the sun is shining. The swells are very large and they don't seem to stop. They seem powerful and more forceful, even after the storm is over, six hundred miles away. It's as if the waves have started very far off and there is an echo. One pushing the other, with one behind a little larger and building. These days are the days that you need to stay in shore and fish for toads!

Birds play a big part, too. If I get up to go fishing and the Pelicans are sitting on the dock or just hanging around, there's a good chance that you'll have strong winds on the ocean. Now, sometimes if you have been feeding those certain Pelicans, they will give you a false reading. You have to get to know your birds!

Another favorite saying of my father was, "They must be walking on the moon again." If there happened to be any bad weather when the shuttle was up, you can believe this might be the problem! When daddy heard of another take off, he would start his talking of fore coming bad weather and high winds. Ninety percent of the time, he did have a point. As I look back, there did seem to be a lot of high winds present after the takeoff.

A fine catch on the Miss Judy Too.

Captain Judy fishing with her friends.

TWENTY-TWO YEARS LATER

When I arrived home the other day, I got a gift. The answer to some questions which I needed badly to fill in the blanks. Mr. Bud Lange of Fort Worth, Texas was standing on my dock. Twenty-two years had passed since we had seen each other. We got to talking and as he started his story I realized who he was. He started by saying, "Do you remember me?" He looked familiar, but I couldn't quite place him. He looked like someone I had seen a short while ago. Well I had.

There was a picture of me and three other fishermen. I had their names, but what I needed was a better copy of the photo that the newspaper had taken. The picture had been in the Savannah Morning News. We had caught thirty plus cobia that day. These fish were seven to eighty pounds.

I shall not long forget that day. It was one of those great days in June, where there wasn't any wind, no waves, and plenty of sunshine. I was still leaving from Captain Walsh's Marina on Lazaretto Creek. I was seventeen, soon to be eighteen. I did not have my captains license yet. I wasn't old enough. I had to be eighteen to even fill out an application. My fishing charter consisted of Bud Lange and his son-in-law, Bob Phipps. They were the first half and the other half was J.B. Nasworthy. My father must have put this party together, the first half did not know the second half until this trip.

As we were departing, there was the usual chatter. Who's going to catch the bigger fish? Well, no one knows for sure. I was just hoping we would at least catch a few big ones!
We were going out to catch cobia. The most liked and one of the strongest pulling fish in the ocean. I made my plans to try the shipping channel. The buoys that mark the channels furnish good places for the fish to hide under. Cobia like to hide under anything that provides shade. Anything just floating or anchored down. It was a known fact that the cobia loved the buoys and the shipping channel. My father had proven this many times. It was where he did his best cobia fishing. It was time for me to make my mark. I had to do good, my party was depending on me. My father had passed on to me all his fishing techniques and secrets. I have to really mess up not to catch anything. Everything seem to be in my favor. It only took about forty minutes

NICE CATCH

Some 30 cobia, the largest of which ran 65-70 pounds, were caught off-shore near the "Texas Tower" by the charter boat "Judy." Judy Helmey, the 18 year old captain of her own boat and daughter of Wilmington Island charter boat captain Sherman Helmey, reported that some of "10 or 11" of the cobia were of the larger type. The successful fishermen pictured with Captain Judy are J.B. Nasworthy, Bud Lange of Fort Worth, Texas, and Bob Phipps.

(Article printed in the Savannah Morning News.)

to get to the area where we would start fishing. Everyone was very anxious to get started.

The first few times we tried, no one was home. Not even a bait fish seemed to be there. As we moved on to deeper water, we started seeing a few hanging around the buoys, but they weren't interested in what we had to offer. We had shrimp, eels, and the greatest lure of all times, the "CISCO KID." We had all the right kinds of bait, but none of them seemed to be working. When daddy used them they always worked. So I guessed sooner or later my baits might work or at least I hoped so.

OK, next buoy. I pulled the boat up alongside the buoy and yes, there were fish. Lots of fish. They kept coming out from under the buoy. Everyone had a fish on at the same time. It was unbelievable! I was running around the boat like a captain without a license... I began gaffing the fish as soon as they were brought to the boat. We had cobia everywhere. I mean everywhere! There were the ones on the deck in the boat and the ones that were still swimming around the boat. There seemed to be an endless amount of cobia in the water. As soon as we boated the ones we had hooked, the hooks were baited and back into the water they went. As soon as the bait hit the water, the cobia jumped on it. As I was waiting for them to pull up their fish, I noticed that all the other cobia, that weren't hooked, were just swimming around the boat what the heck, I'll try to gaff one of these. I did, and it worked. I got the first one, and then a second. I couldn't believe what was happening. Finally, the hooked cobia decided to give it up and they surfaced and I pulled them aboard. As I said before, these fish ranged from seven to eighty pounds. The bigger ones didn't come in too easy. They put up a fierce fight!

Everyone was tired and so was I. We had boated thirty plus cobia. The biggest catch I had ever had! Bud had caught the biggest of all the fish. He was smiling from ear to ear. I was joining him myself with a big smile. I knew my father wasn't going to believe this one. As we were heading home, I started thinking about the day and how it started out so slow. It is amazing how quick things change and boy, do they. I have never caught that many cobias again in one day. I have never seen that many cobias again in one day either!

Needless to say, everyone was very happy! I wish I had a picture of the look on daddy's face when he saw all of the fish. His eyes were as big as saucers! He called up the newspaper and had them rush over to take pictures of what would probably never happen again.

I am so glad we got to meet up again after twenty-two years. Memories are the best. Thanks Bud Lange!

MURPHY'S LAW

We had a ten hour trip scheduled that day. It had promised to be a beautiful day. The sun was shining, calm winds, and a flat. Perfect day for our new customers!

As we were headed offshore, we saw dolphin feeding. All kinds of bait fish and don't forget that beautiful sunrise. It started out to be a pretty normal day.

When we arrived at our destination point, we started fishing for king mackerel. We were having good luck. We were hooking up about every ten minutes. The group was having a great time fighting the fish.

I have been keeping my eye on a line of scattered thunderstorms off to the north. They were, of course, headed in our general direction. Not too unusual for this time of year. Well, the waterspout started dropping out and touching the ocean. They didn't last too long and it wasn't too bad. You're really not in any danger unless you can't get out of their way. I was looking at number nine. It was still before lunch. Everyone was taking pictures and watching as they spun around in our ocean.

Water spouts that haunted us all day.

When number ten arrived, I had no idea it was going to visit so close. The wind started blowing in excess of fifty knots. Too fast! The wind was only in one spot. Our spot! I looked up and there it was, big as day. A funnel dropping down beside us. Ali ran to the helm and very quickly throttled up. Our lines were still out and our customers were all in the cockpit of the boat, including me. We were all thrown on the deck. None of us minded that too much because the funnel landed in our just made wake.

I'd had enough of funnels, rain, and wind. You could call it, A TROLMULSHIS DAY!

I moved inshore and the customers caught a fifty-two pound cuda. We trolled a bit more and decided it was a good time to head home. The weather still didn't look all that good. It still seem to be following us everywhere we went.

After we were underway about twenty minutes, the salt water pump belt broke. I stopped the boat suddenly, very suddenly. Again, everyone that was standing, was not.

I jumped down into the bilge to fix the problem. Ali was busy getting my tools together. I was busy saying a few things and thinking a whole lot more. I was now attempting to put my belt back on.

Ali said "Judy we have a problem." I looked up, probably looking up like a bilge raised rat would look and she said, "We are in the path of a very big and fast sixty-five foot long, triple decker sport fisherman." I thought to myself, surely this vessel has seen us. I mean, we were disabled, not underway, but making way (drifting). I told Ali, "Keep an eye on him." She did and the vessel did not change course! Ali said, "I'm getting the flare gun out just in case." She got the flare gun loaded. The vessel was still bearing down on us. We were now definitely on a collision course. Ali fired once, no change. Again she fired, no change. She shouted "The next one goes in the top station." Just before firing, thank goodness, he finally changed course and pulled to the offshore side of us. Ali sighed, "By the way, the color of the captain's eyes were blue." That's how close he came to hitting us. He must have had his boat on autopilot. Who knows? Maybe his lunch was getting cold...

I got our problem temporarily fixed and off we went. Five minutes into running, the Coast Guard helicopter was hovering over us. This pilot also had blue eyes. They had come to the boat because they thought we were in distress. The Coast Guard is always there if you need them. I quickly radioed in what had happened and why we had discharged the flares. In a matter of seconds, everything was in order. A thumbs up from the Coast Guard and they flew off to save a vessel really in distress.

Well, I was totally worn out by this time. Ali had all she could take and I knew these people were never going to come back again. They probably would never even fish again! We kept heading home.

Three miles from the dock and the stupid belt broke again. This time it broke the temperature gauge wire, electrical wire to the fire extinguisher, and there were several other things I can't mention. "I'll just call for a tow!"

Everyone was standing in the back of the boat. I was, once again, in the bilge and Ali was watching as we drifted with the incoming tide towards home.

I looked up and everyone started laughing. They said, "They had never experienced so much in so little time!" I knew now they would never return. I was wrong with that statement. They did come back and have become very good customers. I am so glad they could take a joke...

Oh, by the way, the name of the party I'm referring to is the Mike Olinger party.

Captain Judy and her first mate Ali holding a king mackerel.

ST ELMO'S FIRE

Several years ago, I was fishing at the snapper banks. It was a cloudy day and it looked like it might rain any second. I had thrown a buoy out on the spot where I wanted to start my drift. We were doing some bottom fishing for snapper and grouper. It was very calm, not a ripple on the ocean. It's so happen that our drift was sort of long so we drifted almost out of sight of the buoy each time. When the fish stopped biting, I would tell the customers to pull their lines in and I would go back to the buoy and we would start another drift. Our buoy was approximately ninety degrees. We were making a westerly drift.

About the fourth time we started back, I looked at my compass and headed back to the buoy. When I had run the amount of time to get back to fishing, I started looking for the marker. I didn't see it! I looked 360 degrees, no markers! I looked back at my wake and I could tell I wasn't exactly heading in a straight line. I wasn't sure what was going on. I told the people to drop the lines. Luckily, I had marked a few hungry fish. I was still looking for that buoy that was hiding from me. No sign of it. Maybe it floated off or maybe the weight had come untied. Who knows?

In the background, I kept hearing these strange popping noises. It was coming from the back of the boat. I started looking for the cause of this noise. It seemed that every time one of the fisherman's rod tip was raised over his head, you heard this popping sound. Where was it coming from? I still hadn't said anything to anybody yet. Well, it's true. If I had said something, what would it have been? Popping noises. Compass is not working. I forgot how to drive. Which one would have been correct? At this point, all of the above...

Captain Ida was on the boat as my first mate that day. I called her to the bow and we very quietly discussed what was going on. In the meantime, I was looking around as I was talking to her and all the metal had turned smoke blue and it seemed to have steam rising from it. The compass was spinning slowly around and around. Then I began to notice that everyone's hair seemed to be standing up. Ida looked funny with all her hair standing up. It looked as though she had stuck her finger in a 220 light socket. We all looked like someone had put us in the dryer and we all had static electricity.

Well, at this point, I am sure I don't know because we just passed into the twilight zone! Ida quickly said that she had read something like this happens to sail boats or boats with masts. However, she had never read anything like what was happening to us now. She said we were under the influence of SAINT ELMO'S FIRE... My next question was, "What?" and of course, "How do we get rid of it?"

We then noticed the popping noise began to get louder. We decided to take down the outriggers and antennas, then lay all the fishing rods down, and just sit there and see what would happen. The force field that had formed around us finally dissipated. I was quite relieved when it happened. Someone up there must be watching out for us. The sun finally came out.

I did a little research on SAINT ELMO'S FIRE. This is the name given to the round flash that can be seen around ships in a thunderstorm. It's actually a charge of electricity caused by the storm. Maybe now, we know why pirate ship's sometimes reported that abandoned ships appeared to be all illuminated. I would have loved to have a photograph of the Miss Judy Too that day!

RIDE THE WILD CATFISH

Have you ever heard about this sport before, NOODLING? Well, I hadn't either until some construction workers doing a job here, chartered my boat and told me of this fun filled sport.

First thing you need to do is find a deep ledge in a pond or river. You dive down either with or without scuba equipment. By the time you finish, you will need scuba equipment. You reach under the ledge and feel for a big catfish, sometimes called a Flat Head Cat. If you happen to stick your hand into his mouth, don't panic, be real still so he will let go. Now, I hope you are following this because you might want to do this one day. OK, now you are there with your hand in the mouth of a thirty to forty pound Flat Head Cat being real still. Right? If you are real still, they say he will eventually unlock his jaws and then you can pull your hand out. Of course, if you are not real still and jerk too soon, then you'll have one arm and hand with some skin missing. Now keep in mind some Northerners say this is a growing sport. I'm still wondering about those Northerners.

Now that you have located the fish you surface. I hope you have some air left! Now you need to take a metal rod with a line on it, go back to the ledge and stick this through his mouth and gills then tie a slip knot. Now all you have to do is pull this catfish out. Simple, right? But if he is mad, he may attack you. I can't see him anything but the fish being mad at this point. You drag him out and he tries to swim off. You hold on until he gets tired or you get tired of being bitten. Your main goal is to make it to the bank. This is called NOODLING.

I will be honest, the reason I have told you about this unusual sport is because I find it very amusing. I tried to vision in my mind what it would be like if I took the before mentioned steps to catch my Flat Head Cat. Well, I don't think I could get off the bank, I would be too busy rolling on the ground laughing...

Captain Judy docking her boat.

SMALL BOATS/BIG FISH

One day while I was out with a charter, we had decided to go over to the Texas Tower to troll for a few Spanish mackerel. While we were trolling around the tower, I noticed a small boat about twenty feet in length tied to the tower. The fisherman in the boat seemed to be alone, I saw no other heads showing. He had several lines out, didn't seem to be having much luck. We weren't either so that made two of us. I can still remember it as if it happened yesterday. The fisherman had a big straw hat on. You know, one of those types that keep the sun off your whole body he was sitting there fishing and I was just trolling around the tower. I was watching him and he was watching me.

Finally he got a hit. It seem to be a fairly good size fish by the way it bent the rod over into the water. He fought this fish for a few minutes and the way it seem to be acting led me to believe it was a big cobia. It hadn't surfaced. Cobia usually stays very deep. By this time, things were getting a little hectic. The fisherman stood up trying to get control of his fish and his hat blew off. It started floating towards and then under the tower. As soon as it cleared the tower, I was going to retrieve it for the fisherman. As I headed for the hat, I saw out of the corner of my eye that he was just about ready to bring his hope to be supper in the boat. Well, to this day, I don't know how he didn't break the line but he pulled the fish into the boat. I might add that the fish seem to be jumping at that time and he might have jumped in the boat. What happened after that was unbelievable!

The fisherman jumped for the engine cover to get out of reach of the thrashing fish. It looked as if the fish might have been forty to fifty pounds. When he landed in the boat it was as if there was an explosion. The fish went wild! The first thing that flew out of the boat was the cooler top, then there were those boat cushions. I could tell that the poor guy in the boat wasn't too happy with his new buddy.

The fish was pitching everything that wasn't tied down and everything that was tied down was being broke or busted. Now he was standing on top of his engine cover watching as this fish trashed his whole boat. I was sure he was hoping this would soon be over. Finally, the fish had decided that he had done enough damage to the boat. He took a leap and jumped back into the water. You have to LOVE the moment! I picked up all this stuff floating around. The cushions, the damaged cooler and top that wasn't even close to being fixable, and one straw hat that will never be the same. I returned all the gear to the fisherman who said, "He probably was too tough to eat anyhow." I cracked up...

King Fish Galore!

DISASTER AT SEA

It was pretty much a normal day. It was six o'clock in the morning, real quiet, and the usual morning noises were all you could hear. Ali Young, my first mate (for over 9 years) arrived, as usual, on time. You could set your clock by that woman. As we were walking down to the boat, we were talking about how we knew it was going to be a wonderful day. The big blues have been biting all week. I call them Choppers. They weigh in at about seven to twelve pounds. They are real fighters and very good to eat. We were supposed to pick our charter party up around seven o'clock at Landings Harbor. It's about a thirty minute ride from my house. The marina is located on Skidaway Island.

We pulled in about 6:45 and started getting ready for the Johnson party. Ali was taking out cigar minnows and squid so it could be thawing. We also had our secret weapon which always puts those blues in a feeding frenzy!

Our party arrived and we were off. As we headed out, the sun was just peeking over the horizon. It was sure a beautiful site. the ocean was very calm. The ocean gulls were having a field day feeding on all the bait that had surfaced. We headed to the L Buoy which is located about fifteen miles east of the Wassaw Sea buoy. This is a manmade reef. There are several pilot boats, barges, and concrete culvert pipe sunk there. Very good fishing. I could see those fish swimming through the culvert pipes now.

We were making about seventeen knots, water splashing at our sides, the engine humming, and the chatter of customers filled the air. When we were about thirty minutes off, the dolphins came swimming up to the boat to sail along the bow. It looked as though they were racing to see which one could get to just the right spot under the bow first. Having the dolphins show up always makes the customer smile. Some of my customers have never seen the ocean much less dolphins screaming to the boat to play in our wake. Their expressions were always delightful.

We finally arrived at the spot. Ali got on the bow and we anchored the boat over the Henry Bacon, a sunken pilot boat located at the L Buoy. usually bait fish will gather around the boat and the blue fish seem to always know there is a free easy meal real close.

We put our lines out and we also put a little of the secret weapon out. It wasn't very long before the Blues were biting everything. Ali was on one side gaffing and I was on the other. The passengers were having a blast!

I had noticed that the sea had started to build. When we left, the waves were about one to two feet, now they were about three to four feet. The ocean seem to be swelling up and all the motion wasn't going in the same direction. I had noticed a temperature change and the wind had started picking up. Not only had it picked up but it had changed directions from the light southeast breeze to a 15 to 20 knot wind out of the northeast. You can believe that if she starts blowing a northeasterly, it will only get worse. The writing was on the wall, she was going to build and blow. I gave it another fifteen minutes and I was sure, at this point, that I was right. The wave height had reached about five feet. The wind was starting to howl. I knew it was time to call it a day…

I explained to Mr. Johnson we needed to leave a little early. I got no complaints, they were very happy. They had already caught their limit, over 50 bluc fish. Ali did her tightrope walk around the bow, holding on with both hands. She turned and looked that look I had seen before. The I think we should have left an hour ago look. Ali tried to get the anchor to release but it was really buried. The waves were now beginning to break. I told her one more try and if we couldn't get it, we would cut the line. Finally, the anchor came loose. Ali, holding on with one hand and pulling with the other finally got it in.

Our heading returning home was about 305 degrees, which would put the wind and waves at my starboard stern. At least I was going to be with the waves, this would help. About twenty minutes after we left, the ocean really started to build. The waves were now about eight foot and better. The Miss Judy Too and her passengers were really being tossed around. There were eight people aboard counting Ali and myself. I knew I would have to get the life jackets out if this continued. The passengers were getting a little uneasy, but at this point, I don't think anyone realized how much danger we were really in. The wind and waves kept building and they were really tossing us around now. We had finally made it within eight miles of the wonderful sea buoy, but eight miles seemed like twenty then! The boat was wallowing about and the waves were now trying to climb into the boat. We had to keep the pumps running constantly.

In shore of me, about three miles, was another serious disaster. A sixty-five foot sport fisherman crewed by a captain and two crew members were heading north. That would put them almost heading directly into the wind and waves. Apparently, the vessel had taken on some water and the pumps were unable to stay ahead of the incoming flow. A wave hit the vessel directly head on. The vessel, being heavy in the water, didn't bounce. She just went deep into the ocean as the wave pushed her over to one side and completely filled every part that wasn't covered. The next wave hit her with fury, rolled into the stern, and took the entire flying bridge off with its occupants inside.

The boat started sinking. It had a raft on the bow that was supposed to inflate but the raft, after inflating became entangled in the bow rail. It only had forty foot of line in which to drift. The fly bridge was swept away. One of the crew members kicked the remaining windows out so it would float. The captain was missing. He was thrown out on impact of the overtaking waves. He was later found dead in his life jacket. The other crew members held onto the bridge parts in hopes that their one "MAYDAY" call was heard by someone.

Well, it did go out. Unfortunately, I wasn't the one who received it. The call was received by the Coast Guard. They acted promptly to assist. All persons involved were picked up. 2 crewmen and one deceased captain.

We weren't out of the weather yet. We were within one mile of the sea buoy and the waves were really pounding at us. We had our lifejackets on hoping that we wouldn't need them. We finally made it to shore line where it seemed we were swallowed up by the land, no more big waves...

Everyone was wet, cold, and tired including me and Ali.

When we arrived at Landings Harbor, Karl, the harbor master, asked if I had seen or heard of a boat sinking. I replied, "NO."

When we arrived home, a good friend of mine, Bill Walsh, called and told me of the tragedy. He told me about the boat sinking and how the raft marked exactly where the boat sank.

It was tangled with the bow rail. The crew members were pushed too far away when the waves hit them to get back to raft.

When we went out the next day, the weather had lifted, the winds weren't blowing and the waves weren't breaking. It was as if nothing had happen, but Ali and I knew that wasn't so. When we got about three miles off the buoy, heading in the same direction as yesterday, there was the raft and below it was a large boat that once floated on top of this ever so calm sea. We had passed right by the raft, right by the people. The pounding ocean and high winds blowing spray across my bow had blinded me from seeing it. All I could think about was if I had seen them, I might have been able to save the captain's life. Both of us just looked over to the area where the raft was floating. No waves, no wind... It's almost like mother nature has a switch she can turn on and off.

We went out with our fishing party, but our thoughts remained on the raft that marked the sunken vessel...

KUNG-FU FISHING

I would like to share with you a great experience I had with three just graduated rangers. None of them were over the age of twenty-one.

They called me up and made a reservation to go out for a day of sun, celebration, and fishing. When they arrived, I had the boat ready and running. In those days, I didn't have a full time mate so it was just them and me.

They had a plastic trash can full of oversized blue ribbon beer. A few pretzels and a bottle of coconut suntan lotion. We loaded up and started off. They seemed very nice. They also seemed very glad to be out among the civilians again. We had the usual conversation on the way out. It was a beautiful day, plenty of sunshine, calm winds, a captain's dream.

When we arrived at our fishing spot, I started showing them how we needed to set up to catch the big ones. We were fishing for cuda, king mackerel, Spanish mackerel, and bluefish. We put out four lines. Two top lines with cigar minnows and two deep lines with silver spoons. I explained that when we had a hook up, I would run back and gaff the fish and put it in the fish box. They seem to go along with that OK. I, also, told them how sharp the fish's teeth were and not to put their hands near the mouth area.
First strike, we had a small cuda hooked up. This fish put up a pretty good fight for his size. I ran to the aft, gaffed the fish, deposited into the box, and back to the helm I went. The guys got really excited with this. They wanted to do the gaffing themselves. I said to myself, "It looks a lot easier than it is."

Next fish was a larger cuda about forty pounds or better. The fish put up a great air show. Leaping and even doing a little Michael Jackson tail walking. When it was time to stick him I yelled, "Get the gaff!" One of the guys looked at me and said, "We don't need a gaff." Before I could get it out of my mouth, he reached down and grabbed the big bad fish. Hooks in mouth, teeth chopping away, he slammed him down on the deck, one chop of the hand broke the fishes neck, end of fight. I was floored and too shocked to speak! At this point, I wasn't sure what would happen next but I was glad I was there to see it. He

153

picked the almost lifeless fish up and put it in the fish box.

The rest of the trip was just as exciting as the first part. We would get hooked up, they would play the fish, grab, slam, chop, and in the cooler it went. They're technique was very much their own. It never crossed my mind to steal their method. All I could imagine is hooks buried in their arms and fish hanging off their ears! They were much quicker than the fish ever thought about being. Thank goodness for that.

We arrived back around three o'clock. We had filled that rather large trash can full of king and Spanish mackerel, cuda and bluefish. They, on the other hand, had helped not only by catching and landing their fish, but by removing the contents of the already full trash can. They traded one for the other.

Back to the barracks to have a fish fry. Which I'm sure they did! Let me tell you how I know about this event...

Five years later, the same three rangers came back to go fishing again. This time, they brought their wives. They had settled down quite a bit. We used the gaff that day and there wasn't a trash can full of beer that disappeared.

The guys told me about the fish fry they had after their first trip with me. They fed quite a lot of rangers. They said that they probably would have had more fish if someone hadn't put a lot of them in the washing machine. I guess they wanted to make sure their fish were real clean...

JUST SAY NO

I know what you are thinking. How can I even write about drugs. I certainly am not supposed to use any of the above mentioned stuff. Well, I don't. However, I have seen a bunch of drugs offshore of Savannah. It comes in different forms. Some is wrapped in burlap bags and marked with the name of a Colombian coffee manufacturer. Some is packaged in plastic and wrapped in Piggly Wiggly Just Say No to Drugs Bags! I have seen a lot more of the stuff on Miami Vice rather than on the ocean, but I have had my share of experiences...

One day, while going to the Savannah snapper banks, I began noticing these large brown bale looking floats. At first, I didn't pay too much attention to them. After I had passed about ten, I started counting these floats as I called them. It wasn't too rough that day, so I left my compass course to get a closer look. Sure enough, it was what I had expected it to be. It was floating high and very light in the water. You could tell that it hadn't been there too long. I took the gaff and stabbed at it a few times and the contents were very dry. I just left it because I had seen enough.

I had a friend who picked up a bale of waterlogged pot once. He said he would never do it again. He spent much time filling out report after report. He said it made him feel like he had done something wrong. So I decided to leave it alone.

There was quite an abundance of it, I guess about thirty-five bales. All these were located in a five mile radius. I guess someone missed there drop. When you are out there alone, you don't know who might show up.

The way I was looking at the situation was this: what if I pick up this stuff and I get boarded by the Coast Guard? Are they going to believe me that I picked up thirty-five bales of pot and was going to turn it in? What if the people who were supposed to pick this stuff up shows up? You got it. We went fishing and forgot about the whole thing!

Another time, I got the chance to see lots of the white stuff up close. Well, I also decided to let it alone and maybe it would find its way to where it belonged. Sure enough, the next day, a charter boat off the South Carolina coast picked up a package containing some cocaine. They did not give their name or any information about it. I would hate to be in their boat shoes!

One foggy morning, I was about thirty miles offshore. Boy, was it foggy. You couldn't see 300 feet in front of the boat. The fog was fading in and out. I would run through patches and then it would clear up for a bit. I got back in the fog again, big time! The sun was just beginning to burn it off some. I kept seeing the reflection of the sun hitting a windshield or maybe a mirror. I proceed with caution and tried to call them on the radio. And yes, I was blowing my foghorn at the right intervals. The closer I got, I began to notice more reflections.

I approached with caution. The sun was really beginning to burn off the fog. I was now seeing more than one boat. I was seeing at least six or seven boats. Not only was I seeing boats, I began seeing a small ship. The boats were around the small ship. I had seen enough. I can guarantee you they weren't fishing. I had definitely seen enough! I was hoping that I hadn't seen too much. I slowly but faintly moved out of that area.

Another interesting adventure that may happen to you when you're a charter boat captain is that people may make unusual requests. They will pay large amounts of money if you go seventy miles offshore and pick up a package off a said ship and bring it back. You might also be asked not to report your boat stolen, at least for three days or until you get the OK.

All this for an unusual amount of cash that comes with all kinds of strings attached. If you decide to do this, your contact then tells you about the strings... Now, while we are stealing your boat, you will be locked in a motel room until this is all over. If everything goes right, then you will get paid. I love listening to all these offers. In fact, I even let them think I might want to go along with them. When I would refuse, of course, they would say "Oh, I was just kidding!" Sure they were...

THE UNDERWATER STALKER

We were fishing one morning at the L buoy (115 degrees off the Wassaw sea buoy). There were only three people aboard that day, John - the one man party, Leon, and me. Leon had worked with my father when he was just 12 or so and now, he was continuing his fishing habit with me. He was my first mate that day. We had been catching a few amberjacks, the fishing was very good. We were using live bait. Spanish mackerel were even working period once in the water, they did not last long period we had boated about five amberjacks, in the 30 to 50 pound range. We were just about to put number six in the boat when we saw something large behind the amberjack. It was the biggest hammerhead I had ever seen!

Leon went to gaff the fish and I hollered for him to stop. The shark was in hot pursuit of our catch. I believe to this day, if I hadn't stopped Leon from gaffing that shark, the gaff and shark would have made contact at the same time, possibly pulling Leon out of the boat. The poor amberjack fearing the boat and the shark was certainly having a slight nervous attack. The fish was tired from fighting and running from the shark. When the shark turned to make his attack, Leon quickly gaffed the fish and brought him aboard. The hammerhead was none too happy. He swam fiercely around the boat looking for its dinner. The shark began darting back and forth trying to pick up on the amberjack. Anything that came in the path of this shark was certainly history... He laid up beside the boat and he sure was every bit of sixteen to seventeen feet long. He was a little half over the length of my 30 foot boat. You know what I am saying, "We need a bigger boat!" Well, we did, and a crane if we have to lift this one out of the water.

I guess the shark had picked up on the distress signals that the amberjack was sending out. When fish are hooked or wounded they put out signals, calls, or waves that sharks and other fish pick up on. They usually head in the general direction for that easy meal.

It has been my experience to have seen more hammerhead's on the surface than other types of sharks. There is a fifty percent chance if you see a shark gliding along the surface, it will be a hammerhead.

I witnessed a very harsh part of Mother Nature and survival of the sea. We watched a small turtle being attacked by a large bull shark. You could see the marks on the turtles back where the shark had his jaws wrapped around his shell. The shark was persistent and kept circling the turtle till he wore him down enough for the main kill. It was sad, but every living creature has to eat something. Sharks, we know, prey on the weak and wounded as often as they can. They are eating machines...

Scottie Edenfield and fishing party showing off bull shark.

SHARK ATTACK

Most sharks probably won't hit an artificial lure. I believe that is because a moving lure does not put off any distress waves that sharks can zeros in on. They are said to have very poor vision and rely mostly on other instincts to lead them to their prey. Fresh oily fish, bloody bonito, or injured live fish are the best crowd drawers. I have seen sharks pick up the scent of blood that has flooded out of the boat scuppers. We have landed bonito, brought them aboard, and have had sharks attack the boat for not being able to get to their intended meal.

One day, while we were fishing off Wassaw Island, an 8 foot tiger shark attacked the stern of the boat. We have him hooked for quite a while, at least an hour. He was quite a long winded fighter. We had him up to the boat several times but we couldn't get him close enough to gaff. The last time we got the shark close, he threw the hook and started swimming off. He stayed on the surface and swam about 50 feet from the boat. The shark turned and headed back in the direction of the boat. I was amazed. He was headed straight for the boat. We all stared in amazement. I wasn't afraid that he could sink the boat or anything; after all, he was only 8 foot. "The nerve of that shark!" Revenge was his motive. He hit the boat, of course, the boat barely moved. He did this a few times and figured out that the fiberglass was a little tougher than he thought. He seemed to be satisfied with what he had done, it swam off, and we never saw it again. We didn't do any swimming that day. Everyone was quite pleased to stay in the boat, even if it was hot...

Hammer heads, to me, are the most unusual of their type. They are not shaped like most of the common types of shark we see in this area. They seem so harmless and they probably are until you come between them and their lunch. They are very large and they don't seem to have to make much movement of their fins to project themselves through the water.

We had a bonito hanging off the side of the boat trying to tease us up a shark. We had tied the bonito to the stern and there were no hooks in the fish. We were just using the bonito as a decoy to bring the shark in close. we had four lines out. Each of them had a fresh Spanish mackerel rigged for shark. We have been waiting for quite a while with no hits, no excitement, and no fins showing. The bonito was just hanging there. In fact, everyone was about asleep or daydreaming about the big one that hadn't showed up yet. I was sitting on the flybridge just staring out doing my own daydreaming. I guess you could say I was about to go asleep myself when out of the corner of my eye I thought I saw something. I did. I saw it again, sure enough, it was that fin we were looking for.

This shark had picked up on the scent of the bonito. The shark appeared to be ready to attack and eat as soon as possible. Right before a shark attacks its prey, the shark starts darting towards its victim, but doesn't attack right off. He's just getting into the mode to do so. Well, this shark was in that mode right now! We had four lines out. Two lines without even pulling out any drag were both cut as if someone had a knife down there and they were using it.

The shark then approached the boat; he was truly ready for something more than just those small mackerel. The bonito was still hanging over the side. I didn't realize how short the lines were between the fish and boat until CRASH!!! The shark had jumped up and grabbed the bonito. I have never seen so much crashing the bait so close to the stern of my boat before. Everybody's heart had to be racing, I know mine was!

My first mate, Scottie, grabbed the line that held the fish and started to pull it towards the boat. This hammerhead had half the fish in his mouth and he was determined to get the other half. Scottie looked like a dishrag flopping in the wind. I yelled, "Let go, let them have it, back up!" If Scottie had slipped and fell overboard, that would have been it for him, I'm sure. He dropped the line and the shark continued to rip at the bonito. He had gotten half of the fish but was persistent in getting the rest. Everyone at the start of the boat was soaked. Water was splashing from every direction. The shark finally got what he wanted, which was the rest of the fish.

It was silent for a few seconds then the third line went off. That only lasted a second, the line cut. We had one more line left and you guessed it, he took it. Well, this time he got the bait and not the line. The shark took off in a northerly direction headed for deep water. We had 600 yards online. I was hoping to have time to release my anchor and follow this bad boy. He was quite a large scalloped hammerhead. He looked to be over 14 feet long, a big fish. Everyone was scurrying around doing their job. The line was peeling off so fast, I couldn't believe it! The fish just kept the pressure on and the line was quickly leaving the school. I knew we didn't have a chance. The fish was doing some traveling now, fast as the seconds went on. When the line came to the end of the spool, I knew what was going to happen. There was no way to get the boat turned around so I could chase this shark. Well it did come to an end, and with a bang. The line popped off the spool and shot through the rod tips, but when it got to the last rod tip the line took the whole end of the rod off. I mean it made a heck of a noise. It sounded like a 380 being shot into the air.

Well, we all stood there in amazement. We all knew what we all had seen. Everyone was sort of speechless. I know I was. Poor Scottie had rope burns to prove his encounter with it that shark. I had a broken rod and a reel that would never be the same. And well, our customers will have a story to tell that will last forever...

Captain Judy and Captain Ali holding shark.

Bottom fishing is another good time that sharks might show up. When you're pulling up the bottom fish, they send off distress signals that sharks home in on. They pick up the fact that there is an injured fish in the area and they head for that area. With six people fishing at once, there are a lot of distress signals being sent out. The signals are being sent out in a continuous motion from around 100 feet to the surface. It will bring in the big boys, looking for that free meal or easy meal. Usually, the sharks will come right to the surface following the fish, hoping to get a bite.

When we spot these sharks, if the customers want shark steaks for supper, then this is how we go about it. If the shark comes directly to the boat, all you have to do is throw him a rigged fish and usually he will take it and run. Give him a chance to sink his teeth into it, getting down to the hooks, and then set the hook. Now, if the shark seems to be aware of the boat and doesn't want to come close, you can always pull the boat up ahead of his intended direction and throw the bait into his path. This usually works real well too.

Another way is to throw a can out and the noise usually from the can hitting the water will bring the shark closer. They are very curious fish. I am not telling you to litter. You can pick up the trash later. I have even had the shark attack the can and swallow it. It depends on which mode the fish is in.

Anyway, as he is approaching the can, throw the bait out at the fish and let it sink. If none of the above fit your situation, hit the shark with the bait. Maybe his skin sensors will pick up on the taste of the bait, which could possibility put them into a feeding mode.

I have had sharks attack the boat. I have had them attack cans. I have had them attack themselves. They will even try to eat their own guts if they are hanging out. We dropped a shark over-board by mistake when we were trying to gut it, while still alive, he swam around in circles trying to eat his own guts. I have had them jump out of the water to go after bait that was hanging over the side. I've had them get the bait they jumped up for and get hooked in the same process. One day, we caught two small school sharks this way. I learned that day, never to hang any bait over the side anymore. Even you have heard me say, "Sharks have bad eyesight." I began wondering that day if this is true.

They certainly have a good sense of smell if they are truly half blind. Remember all this information I am giving you are things that have actually happened to me. These are not stories I have sat here and made up. I don't believe some of them myself and I was present.

We use to catch a lot of small sharks, less than twenty pounds, in the Wilmington River and in the mouth of Wassaw Sound; but, with the increasing food value and more people targeting the species, the shark population is down considerably. So if you catch a shark or any other fish and you're not going to eat it, please release the fish for another day...

Dun Funderbuck and friend holding black tip shark.

Captain Judy gripping a sand shark.

THE SEA MONSTER

I first came into contact with a Sand Bar Tiger when I was fishing at the Barnstable. We had been fishing for amberjack and Barracuda. We were using Spanish mackerel for bait which we had caught that day. The live ones were working the best. They got the quickest results. There is nothing better that a cuda or amberjack likes than a chase. We had put quite a few fish aboard. The action was good. As usual, the bite slowed down. They had been biting all morning. I figured it was time for them to slow up. We had one more live mackerel, so we put it out. We waited for our next victim to attack. This only takes a moment, however, this time nothing was even looking at the bait. We waited patiently for something to take it.

It was around eleven o'clock in the morning. At the beginning of the charter, the party had asked if I had been catching any sharks. My remark was we had been catching a few sand sharks, which was very normal for this time of the year. They had brought their nephew, Joey Ingentio, so he could have a chance at catching a shark. All of Joey's uncles had planned this trip so that he could try his luck at shark fishing. They were golf players and only came along for the ride.

We were all talking about different types of fish. We had already had a great day, but no sharks. My first mate, Ali, kept watching the line. We still have our live Spanish mackerel out waiting for the big one to bite. I figured that a cuda or amberjack would take it first, but I was hoping for a shark.

The line began to move slowly out. It seemed as if someone was down there was jerking the line and playing a trick. Ali picked up the rod to set the hook, she knew it wasn't a cuda or amberjack. She set the hook, nothing. She free spooled back to the fish, he picked it up again. This time she let him swallow it down to his navel. This time she set the steel to him. It was a good hook. The fish began to peel off line as fast as it could go. I knew I had only seconds to get the boat headed in that direction. I would be out of line shortly, like in the next second! I finally got the boat turned around and we chased and chased this sea monster, never getting a chance to see it. Two hours went by and Joey was still at the rod maintaining. He was doing a great job he was very determined to get this fish in on his own.

Ali was standing in the cockpit with her standard three foot gaff. The line did surface. The fish was finally going to surface. Well, he did. It was a ten foot Sand Bar Tiger Shark. Ali looked up at me with her now real small gaff and said, "You have got to be kidding!" Well, we weren't, we got our shark tools ready. We had one five foot stainless gaff with a heavy rope attached to the boat. Then we had several more gaffs that would enable us to pull in this sea monster. It was going to be a family affair...

We still had a while before this shark would surface again. We would have to really tire this one out if we hope to land it. Everyone was getting a turn at the shark. We had almost three hours already on this shark. He was starting to weaken a little. We had already weakened. About the time it looked like we were going to get our chance to gaff him, the rod butt broke off and off he went again on another trip to the bottom! Now Joey had a real problem. We still had the fish and what was left of the rod. The rod was very hard to hold. This doubled the tension on his arms.

Joey Ingentio holding open the mouth of his sand bar tiger shark.

Finally, the fish did surface. Joey trying to reel him close so we can get a chance to gaff him. We did gaff him, but he rolled off the gaff, so I shot him and that only made him madder than before. He took off! We brought him to the boat several times and I shot him again. Finally, I could tell we were going to get the chance we needed to gaff him. Ali got the gaff to stick. She stuck it down his throat. With this move the shark finally gave up. The shark was dead we tied it to the stern. It had been four hours since we had hooked this shark. Everyone was terribly exhausted!

We had to put this shark in the boat. It was clear we could not do it ourselves. We had to enlist some of our other riders aboard to help. We gave everyone a gaff. I had the tail tied to the boat. All we had to do was pick the sea monster up and bring him aboard, right? Sounds easy, huh? Well, it would seem so.

We were going to try to lift him up on the stern. I gave Ali go ahead and the shortest gaff by mistake. We all tried to lift the shark that was dead, or at least we thought was dead. This creature let out a loud ROAR, that was unbelievable and then he started thrashing from his head to his tail! Everyone let go quickly and jumped back. Now you know why I had tied the tail to the stern. I pulled the shark backwards for a few minutes I was sure he was gone this time! We started trying to pick him up again. Finally, we got the strength to pull him on the stern. He was much larger than we had first suspected. He looked like he weighed close to 270 pounds, he was a definite MONSTER.

We started home from our journey. Everyone was tired, covered with blood from the shark, and smell like a human shark! On the ride home, I tried to decide how we were going to butcher this shark. We arrived at home and put him on the dock. We tried cutting but it was a little slow. Then I remembered I had a two man tree saw. We got it and it worked much better, we cut the shark up into four large pieces. We put the meat in coolers and iced it down. We put the head, fins, and tail in one cooler. We all looked as if we had been to the slaughterhouse. I reminded everyone to be sure not to put their soiled clothes in their suitcases. The smell would only continue to get worse as the hours flew by.

They did listen to what I had said. They took their clothes off and threw them into the trash. I didn't mean they couldn't get the smell out. I heard one guy say to the other as they left, "I thought I got plenty of exercise golfing, but wrestling a shark dead or alive is definitely a total workout!"

SOUNDS FROM THE DEEP

I have had lots of fun trips to the Gulf Stream. In fact, I think I could say that every trip I took was exciting! I guess being out that far has a certain effect on a person. I know it did on me. You know the saying, "The bigger the pond, the bigger the fish." Well, that is true, at least when you are talking about the ocean as a pond. The water is so blue and clear you think you ought to be able to see the bottom. We did mostly bottom fishing on the edge and trolling in the Gulf Stream. We would leave early in the morning and arrive about noon. We would anchor up around eight o'clock at night and stay at anchor till about six o'clock the next morning.

Upon our arrival, we would start hunting for some good bottom so we could start bottom fishing. The depth of the water was about 200 feet. A long way to reel up to 16 ounce sinkers. When fishing in the stream area, you really never knew what you might catch; but you could be sure of one thing, it would be a large size! I guess the best grouper day we ever had was when we got into the snowy grouper. At first, I called them old yellow mouth grouper, but that was just my name for them. We must have caught several hundred pounds that day.

Sonny Carter and J.T. from Hazelhurst had chartered the boat for this trip. In fact, I believe he had chartered two boats on this trip. Sonny was a good, hard fisherman. If a grouper was there, he was sure to get him. You can believe that Sonny and J.T. had a hundred dollar bet on who was going to catch the biggest fish. Well, they got their share of them that day. I know we caught over thirty large grouper that day. It was fun, but trying to get them to the surface was a lot of work. It seem to take a long time. I know, I caught a few myself. It was just about dark when the grouper stopped hitting and believe me, everyone was tired.

I pulled over to a spot I had looked at earlier. It seem to be covered with all types of fish. With a little luck, those who wanted to fish could at least still catch a few while we waited for daylight. I myself was real tired. I wanted to lay my head down and forget about big yellow grouper. Scottie was on the boat with me that trip. He was ready to fish all night, of course, he did. I laid down and tried to get some shuteye. When I retired, Sonny and Scottie were fishing away at the stern. They both were catching big vermilion snapper and triggerfish. They seem to be having a blast. Everyone else in the party had also thought that taking a little nap was a good idea. When I am at the stream, I sleep with one eye open and the other eye closed. There is something so quiet about being out there. If you listen, there are sounds I'm not sure how to describe. I call them big fish sounds coming straight from the deep!

I have been laying down for probably about two hours, when I heard all this noise from the back of the boat. You guessed it, Scottie and Sonny had hooked into something BIG! I jumped up and could see both of them jumping around in the cockpit. Scottie was screaming, "HIT HIM, HIT HIM!" I jumped up to see what they were trying to hit and boy, was I surprised! They had caught two of the largest EELS I have ever seen! They were jumping, flopping, and rolling around as Scottie tried to calm them down. These eels were every bit over 20 pounds each. They were over 4 feet long. I was too shocked. The guys finally got control of the deck back. I mean the eels had it for a while. Sonny cut the eels up and took them home. He said he had them before and that they tasted good. Well, I guess he had plenty to try different ways.

I was wide awake now. It was about 4:00 o'clock in the morning. We had a light hanging over the side of the boat all night. It had attracted some really strange company. Let's see, we had dancing squid, big lip trigger, and we had some other silverfish that were swimming around in a circle. I could see ships in the distance, it was so peaceful...
Around 6:00 o'clock that morning, we pulled anchor and started our new fishing day. We had a good six hours of fishing left to enjoy. I looked around the old yellow hole and they had checked out or either we had caught them all. This is highly unlikely. So, we tried elsewhere. I found a little spot. We dropped our lines and sure enough, everyone got a fish on. We had found the strawberry patch. We were pulling in strawberry grouper, six at a time. They really do look like a strawberry skin, deep red with little gold spots. Well, we finally groupered it out. We had filled up all the coolers and it was time to head home. I was glad, I was tired and really wanted to get going in that direction. It was a great ride the seas were calm and the sun was shining. What a great life I lead...

Sonny and J.T. chartered of the boat a lot to go to the Gulf Stream. In fact, they were some of my best customers. I think they would have stayed a week, if I would have let them.

I will never forget the time I wandered into an area off the coast, about 70 miles offshore, that is strictly off limits for us fishing people. The armed forces are the only ones allowed in this area. I use to wonder why. Now, I know why! They played their war games there. Believe me. It is true! I must have just been on the edge of that area, but believe me it was too far. Here comes aircraft carriers, destroyers, submarines, and aircraft. I thought World War III had started. I looked like a dot compared to these ships. I wasn't as big as their lifeboats!

Needless to say, I was out of there as quick as I got in there. I was escorted...

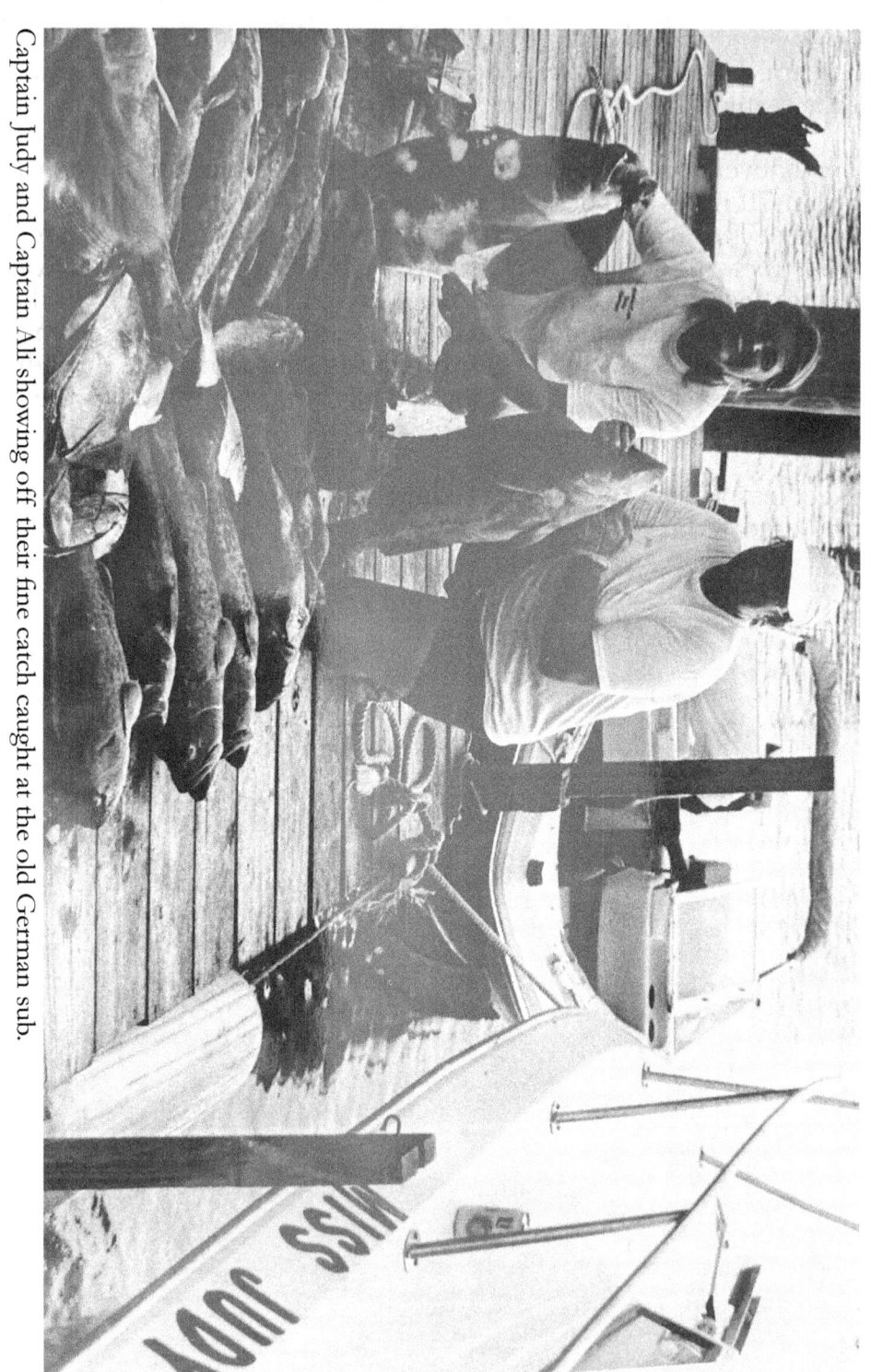

Captain Judy and Captain Ali showing off their fine catch caught at the old German sub.

CAPTAIN JUDY'S RECIPES

STUFFED RED SNAPPER
red snapper
salt, pepper
onion salt
garlic powder
6 bacon strips
sliced lemon
2lb crabmeat
medium onion
2 eggs
1 tube of crushed saltines
Dill

With the new laws we have today, the average size red snapper you can keep is 7 pounds. With this recipe you should be able to serve six.

When you clean your fish: just scale and gut him. You can remove his head if you like. I don't. If you leave the head on, you need to remove his gill plates. Those are the red plates located right inside the throat of the fish. Please remove the eyes and replace with an olive or cherry.

Line your pan with aluminum foil. Grease the foil, so the fish won't stick. Lay your fish in the pan. Season with salt, pepper, garlic powder, and onion salt. Season inside and out. Put two slits on the side facing up. Now you are ready to stuff your fish.

Mix your crab meat, beaten eggs, chopped onion, saltines, pepper, and salt. Stuff this in the cavity of fish. It will be more than your fish will hold, put it all around the cavity.

Lay bacon and lemon on fish, lightly sprinkle with dill. Put in preheated oven, 350 degrees and bake covered for one hour, remove cover to brown.

GRILLED KING MACKEREL OR SHARK STEAKS

6 mackerel steaks
2 bottles of the cheapest French dressing you can find
garlic powder
salt
pepper

Marinate steaks in mixture of dressing, garlic powder, salt, and pepper. You can get away with only four hours, I do it overnight period the flavor really sets in.
Spray your grill with Pam and put the steaks directly on the grill. Baste them with mixture. Cook one side until steaks are white halfway through and then turn them over.
I have substituted the French for Italian dressing. It works well also. good

GOT MORE BOOKS!!!....

If you would like to have additional copies of this book <u>My Father The Sea and Me</u> please give us a call at 912 897 4921 or email fishjudy2@aol.com or judyhelmey@gmail.com.

Our mailing address and location:

Captain Judy Helmey
Miss Judy Charters
124 Palmetto Drive
Savannah Georgia 31410

Captain Judy's Kicking Fish Tail Since 1956! Inshore Fishing Techniques is also available as well as other books that are in the process of being published!

Thanks for reading!
Captain Judy

Before

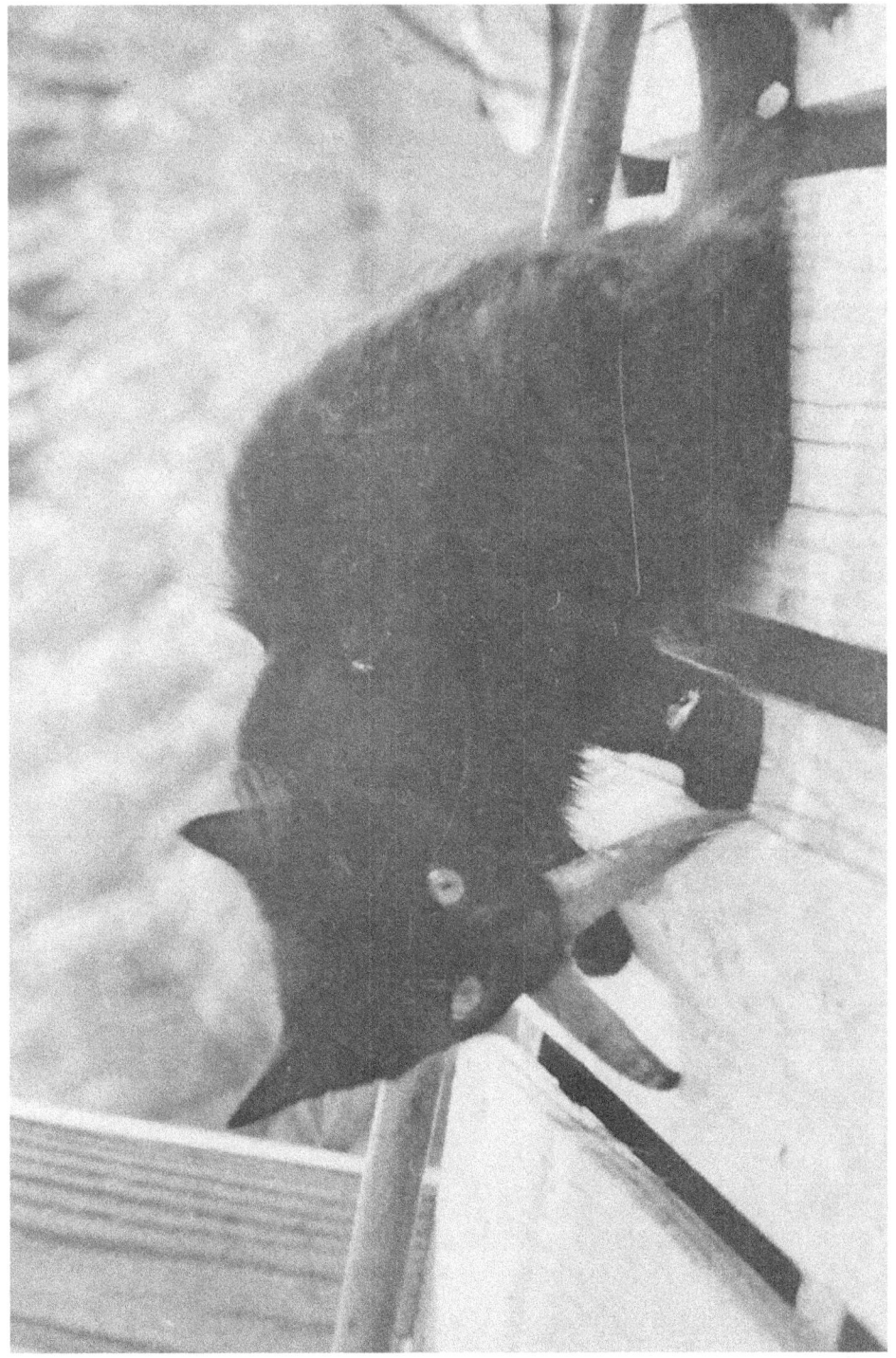

After   "The End"

www.ingramcontent.com/pod-product-compliance
Lightning Source LLC
Chambersburg PA
CBHW061751120626
46550CB00005B/1955